INTO THE
DEEP

DISCOVERING YOUR TRUE
Relationship with Jesus Christ

BETHANY LENTZ MURDOCK

Into the Deep: Discovering Your True Relationship with Jesus Christ

Trilogy Christian Publishers A Wholly Owned Subsidary of Trinity Broadcasting Network

2442 Michelle Drive Tustin, CA 92780

Rights Department, 2442 Michelle Drive, Tustin, CA 92780.

Trilogy Christian Publishing/TBN and colophon are trademarks of Trinity Broadcasting Network.

For information about special discounts for bulk purchases, please contact Trilogy Christian Publishing.

Trilogy Disclaimer: The views and content expressed in this book are those of the author and may not necessarily reflect the views and doctrine of Trilogy Christian Publishing or the Trinity Broadcasting Network.

Manufactured in the United States of America

10 9 8 7 6 5 4 3 2 1

Library of Congress Cataloging-in-Publication Data is available.

ISBN: 979-8-88738-976-9 | E-ISBN: 979-8-88738-977-6

DEDICATION

This book is dedicated and offered back to Jesus. He has carried me through so many deep waters and given me only more and more of Himself. So I offer this work back to Him who is the same, yesterday, today, and forever. "So is my word that goes out from my mouth: It will not return to me empty, but will accomplish what I desire and achieve the purpose for which I sent it" (Isaiah 55:11, NIV).

ACKNOWLEDGMENTS

To my husband, Paul, who has cheered this book on in me, told me I could write and believed in the message from the start; I love you with all of my heart.

To my beautiful parents, Steve and Cathy Lentz, who gave me Jesus and set the pattern for me on what it looks like to go deeper with Him in all circumstances and have never wavered.

To my brother and sister-in-law, Carl and Laura Lentz, who have stood at my side in dark days and not allowed my flame to go out.

To my sisters, Mary and Corrie Lentz, who I love dearly and who have walked with me from the start and been my first friends. Thank you for praying for me and giving me hope.

ENDORSEMENTS

We were created through relationship and for relationship with God and others. *Into the Deep* lovingly and passionately invites the reader to a journey of profound intimacy with the Creator. As with any adventure, much like a ship launching into open waters, there are challenges and perhaps even fears to overcome but also the joy of experiencing Him in new and unexpected ways. Bethany Murdock captures the heart of God while calling the believer to a deeper trust and place of surrender. Harbors provide safety and comfort, but they are not what ships were built for.

— Eric Scalise, PhD, Author, Speaker, and Licensed Therapist, Sr. Vice President and Chief Strategist with Hope for the Heart

If you've been standing on the shoreline, paralyzed by your fear and talking your way out of God's calling, *Into the Deep* reminds us we serve a limitless God. A God who is ready to show us a destiny beyond what we can ask or imagine. Bethany shows us how to take those first steps into the great unknown. And, eventually, how to wade fearlessly into the deep waters of faith, freedom, and absolute fulfillment in Jesus.

— Paula Faris, Founder and President of Carry Media, Former ABC News Anchor and Correspondent, Good Morning America Weekend Anchor, Former Cohost of The View, and Author

MY PRAYER FOR YOU...

Lord Jesus,

I pray that in the heart of every person who reads the words of this book, You would place courage. Courage to follow You into deeper places than they have ever been before. Let formerly shallow roots grow deep and strong in You. God, let that same power that raised Christ Jesus from the dead be present in each life. I pray for an outpouring of the Holy Spirit over Your people across the earth. I ask for hunger for Your Word to cause the empty to be filled, the sick to be made well, and the broken to be made whole. I pray for the signs and wonders promised in Your Word to follow those who believe in You worldwide. Teach us to move in the Spirit! Thank You for Your invitation to know You more and the promise that if we seek You, we will find You!

In Jesus' name, I pray.

Amen

TABLE OF CONTENTS

INTRODUCTION

There is something about deep water that scares most people. This is especially true for anyone who has not yet learned how to swim. If you can't swim, just being near the water can often be terrifying. For a non-swimmer, the water means trouble, and the deep water means danger. Then there are those people who love to point out where the deep water is. "Be careful; it gets deep right there," or "You better turn around; you're getting close to the deep end!" And if you have ever been out in a boat with a group of people on a large lake or perhaps even the ocean, someone in-variably says, "The dark water is where the drop-off happens, and that's where it gets really deep…" These people mean well, but their comments tend to charge the atmosphere with the ominous possibility of danger. Again, a warning of doom. Words like "dark water" and "drop-off" only add to the terror of the deep and can be so intimidating!

Sadly, this is where it all begins: the belief that "deep" is dangerous and that it should be avoided at all costs! I find it interesting that it is from this very place, this point of impending danger and doom, that two completely different personality types emerge: the "risk taker" (the adventurous type) and the "safety zoner" (the cautious type). The risk taker is that person who seemingly laughs in the face of danger. They tend to thrive on the possibility of disaster. The safety zoner is the type of person who is more cautious and reserved. They tend to shrink back from the edge of anything that even resembles trouble, while the risk taker runs right up to the edge. Some even run up to and jump off the edge in that risky rush, screaming as they go! The risk taker is viewed in an almost irresponsible and daring light, while the safety zoner is viewed as responsible and smart. What fascinates me is that these same classifications can be carried over into our life with God, especially the safety zoner. These unwritten definitions begin to define who we are as spiritual people. They can even limit our spiritual growth and hinder our spiritual lives, causing us to become a prisoner to our very own personalities! Before we know it, our lives become centered on the comfortable and also on what is known or who we "are" versus what we can *become* through Jesus Christ.

We are content with the expected and move away from the unexpected. We become routine, and in the process, we never experience the POWER that comes from choosing to follow God into the deeper places in Him. I believe that we are living in important days. Days that require God's people more than ever to be courageous and bold, to be strong in Him! I also believe that the kind of lives Jesus died to give us are ones that are full of power and expectation! These are days when Jesus is moving and calling us to stand up against the fear that keeps us from taking ground and pushing through to KNOW Him at a deeper level.

You may be asking the question right now, "What does that even mean, to go 'deeper' with God?" and "If I want to go deeper in God than I am today, how do I do it?" As you turn the pages of this book and we walk through this thought together, *into the deep,* my prayer for you is that you would gain greater insight into how to truly discover your personal relationship with Jesus Christ. The kind of relationship that He has in mind for everyone who calls upon His name.

Whether you have accepted Jesus decades ago, you have only recently made a decision to follow Jesus, or are still on the fence about who He is to you, His desire for you is the same! That desire is that you would "draw near to God and He will draw near to you" (James 4:8, NIV). This desire is the starting point for finding your way to more of Jesus. I have also found that this same desire that is our starting point is also the returning point for us our whole life long. If we keep coming back to draw near to Jesus, He will always respond!

I realize that for some of you reading this book, even the word "relationship" is one that you may struggle with in some way because of your own life experiences up to this moment. Maybe you have never had a good relationship with your own father or mother, or perhaps you experienced a lack of care and concern from a mother or husband or wife. Maybe every relationship you have ever known has left you feeling disappointed or used, and you feel "disqualified" or "unworthy" for the journey. I want to especially encourage you that you are so loved by Jesus! You are more than welcome by God to come to deeper places regardless of where you have already been. Colossians 1:12 (AMP) reminds us of this truth: "Giving thanks to the Father, who has *qualified* us to share in the inheritance of the saints (God's people) in the Light." God's healing power will meet you wherever you are right now. I can promise you that you will not regret stepping out and reaching out to God in a deeper way.

If you want more of Him, if you are thirsty and hungry for more of His power at work in your life, then this book is written just for you! It is the desire of God that you would be filled in a fresh way every single day. Yesterday's power won't fuel today! We need fresh power for each day of our lives. There is a sameness in which I believe the devil wants every Christian to be bound. A place where there is no stepping out, no expectation, and as a result, we find ourselves splashing around in shallow water near the shore!

The GOOD news is that it doesn't have to be this way! No matter what has happened in your life up until this very moment, there IS more! Even if you have been on the shore for some time, today can be the day you make the change and ask for MORE. It simply means that you are willing to make the choice to follow Jesus, no matter what, wherever and however He chooses to lead. The heart of God is that we would KNOW Him and BELIEVE Him (Isaiah 43:10). Unbelief is one of the greatest ways to stay right where we are and never truly press IN to all God has called us to! When we choose not to just know God in theory, and we instead get a personal revelation of WHO He is, it is easy to step out into uncharted waters with Him at our side.

Let's face it, most of us, if we are being honest, like to know what to expect. I happen to be one of those people! I feel like I function best if I can "prepare" and "plan" for whatever the situation might demand. My natural personality doesn't really love spontaneous or unplanned or unorganized situations! I really don't like being caught off guard. So, I'm sure you can imagine how much God has had to rock my world in all kinds of ways to keep me from "planning" and "preparing" HIM right out of it! The truth of the matter is, God moves in just this way more often than not. He intentionally leaves gaps so we can watch Him show Himself strong.

In 1988, I had an experience that forever changed my relationship with God. I was in the seventh grade, living in suburban Chicago, when I began to realize that I could experience the power of God for myself. One Wednesday night, I was in a youth service, and the presence of God was very strong as we worshiped and sang. The worship went on longer than usual because there had been a shift that night in the atmosphere. The words we were singing rose up inside my heart. A fire was catching as we sang what is now a very old song yet still resonates with me today, "Here I am, send me to the nations, as an ambassador for You, as an ambassador for You, Here I am!" It hit me that I could actually BE someone God would want to use! We worshiped, and then the worship changed to prayer. Then we began to flood the altar of the church and fell on our knees as we cried out for God to pick US, to choose US, to move through US!

The front of the church and altar area became crowded as hundreds of young people, just like me, raced to the front. Those who were down front initially had to move up to the empty choir loft to make room for the surge of people. Everyone who came forward that night cried out to God for MORE of His presence. I could hear the prayers of the people around me asking Jesus, in their own very personal way, to set their hearts on fire. What began as a low hum of self-conscious prayer in the room turned into bold, powerful declarations of faith as the Holy Spirit swept through that meeting! I remember not wanting to leave that service! Parents began to show up in the auditorium to see what was happening because no one was coming OUT at the normal time to head home!

When I finally did go home that night, I was very quiet in the car as I continued to sense that something had happened in my heart. I was different. I really KNEW that my life was going to be used by God and that He had just invited me to a MEASURE-LESS PLACE. It was a place I had never been to before, and all I knew was that I wanted to go wherever He was going! Everything in me wanted to know the power of God like I had experienced it that night. Something changed in me that night and what I believed about the life I could have in God!

Over and over again since that moment in the seventh grade, I've heard God speak to my spirit, "I raised *you* up for this very purpose, that I might display my power in you and that my name might be proclaimed in all the earth" (Romans 9:17, NIV). In other words, "I have a work I would like to do through YOU so that many will come to know me and there will be praise and honor brought to MY name because of it!" As God has given me more and more revelation on this thought throughout the seasons of my life, I've come to know and believe that I haven't been saved and raised up to live in the predictable out of FEAR of the unknown! There have been moments where the devil has tried to quench that flame of hunger that started so many years ago in me to follow Jesus at a higher, deeper level. That's what he does! The devil tries to put out any fire that moves us to action in God by setting before us the option of a "safe" and "quiet" life that no longer hungers to follow Jesus into the deep!

There is WORK to be done in the kingdom, and we all have a part to play. The problem is while we are busy on the shore, deciding whether or not to get involved, lives hang in the balance! There really is no time to waste. I love Isaiah 43 in The Message Bible; it has been a lifeline to me throughout the years as I have entered my own deep waters.

> But now, God's Message, the God who made you in the first place, Jacob, the one who got you started, Israel: "Don't be afraid, I've redeemed you. I've called your name. You're mine. When you're in over your head, I'll be there with you. When you're in rough waters, you will not go down. When you're between a rock and a hard place, it won't be a dead end—Because I am God, your personal God, The Holy of Israel, your Savior."
>
> **Isaiah 43:1–4 (MSG)**

Isn't it comforting to know that our amazing God promises to be with us when we face life's challenges? By the way, He never said we wouldn't go through times of trouble. There are times in each of our lives when we will pass through waters or go through flames. But God declares that He will be with us.

The promise at the outset of this book is that Jesus IS with us! He is near to those who draw near to Him. So, drowning isn't an option as we follow Him INTO THE DEEP!

CHAPTER 1

THE MEASURELESS PLACE

So, you've been a Christian for a while, or maybe you have just made a decision to follow Jesus, or maybe you have never made a commitment to give Him your life, but have you ever thought, "Now what? What do I do after I receive Jesus? What comes next?" Have you ever wondered how to have a deeper relationship with Jesus Christ? Have you met people that seem to be experiencing a life in God that you wish you had, or do you wish you knew how to tap into that deeper life? Well, I have great news for you! You *can* have a relationship that is deep, meaningful, and fulfilling with Jesus Christ! The truth is God has wanted this kind of relationship all along! When God said, in Genesis 1:26 (NIV), "Let us make mankind in our image, in our likeness," He was looking for relationship. And later, Genesis 3:8–9 states that God was walking in the garden in the cool of the day and looking for Adam and Eve, whom He created. Verse 9 reads that God was calling for them. Why? Why would He do that? Relationship! It's what He was after when He said, in the book of Jeremiah, "'Israel, out looking for a place to rest, met God out looking for them!' God told them, 'I've never quit loving you and never will. Expect love, love, and more love!'" (Jeremiah 31:2–6, MSG). He was looking for relationship! And guess what? He is still walking through the garden in the cool of the day, even today; He is looking for you and calling out your name! He wants relationship!

Many of us make the decision to make Jesus our Lord and Savior, but short of that, we have no idea how to live the new life we have been given on this side of heaven (the here-on-earth side) and experience the life of God that happens here beyond that decision. After all, Jesus Himself said that He came "that they may have life, and that they may have it more abundantly" (John 10:10, NKJV).

The starting point for our own journey with God begins when we take the limits off of what God can do for us, how He is going to do it, when He will do it, and why He chooses the methods He uses! The limitations we place on God come more often than not from our own experiences and even our own preferences. We make decisions on the *way* we will "allow" God to be present in our lives; usually, this is based on what *we* can understand or think *we* can handle! Yet, this is the root of our problem! This problem of putting limitations on God obstructs and can even prevent us from seeing WHO Jesus really is. Our measuring lines are what hold us back. When we take the limits off and we put our measuring lines down, we go to the launching place for a deeper relationship with Jesus, the measureless place. It is right here that we release God to take us somewhere we have never been before.

Most of us, if we are being honest, like to know what to expect. I happen to be one of those people! I feel like I function best if I can "prepare" and "plan" for whatever the situation might demand. My natural personality doesn't love spontaneous or unplanned or unorganized situations! I really don't like being caught off guard. It is almost impossible to surprise me! Every surprise birthday party that has ever been planned for me, I have known about. I have ways of finding these things out! (Sorry to everyone who has ever tried to plan something for me! (Now you know!)

So, I'm sure you can imagine how much God has had to rock my world in all kinds of ways in order to keep me from "planning" and "preparing" HIM right out of it! The truth of the matter is, God, more often than not, moves in just this way. He leaves gaps on purpose, so we can watch Him show Himself strong.

We Wanted MORE!

In 1988, I had an experience that forever changed my relationship with Jesus Christ. I was in the seventh grade, living in suburban Chicago, when I began to realize that I could experience the power of God. I was in a youth service, and the presence of God was very strong as we worshiped and sang. The worship went on longer than usual because there had been a shift that night in the atmosphere. Something had changed. What started out as a normal youth service turned into an "open heaven" moment! There was a different hunger in the room; people came in expecting that God would move. The people in that meeting actually wanted the power of God, and there was a sense that no one was leaving without it! As we worshipped, the words we were singing rose up inside my heart. A fire was catching as we sang what is now a very old song, but the words are still important! We sang, "Here I am, send me to the nations, as an ambassador for You, as an ambassador for

You, here I am!" Those words exploded inside of me! Suddenly, it hit me that I could actually BE someone God would want to use! We continued to worship, and then the worship changed to prayer. We all began to flood the altar of the auditorium, and on our knees, we cried out for God to pick US, to choose US to move through!

The altar became full of literally hundreds of young people my age. There were so many of us that we started moving up into the empty choir loft to make room for more people to come forward and ask God for MORE. I could hear the prayers of the people around me asking Jesus, in their own very personal way, to set their hearts on fire. What began as a low hum of self-conscious prayer in the room turned into bold, powerful declarations of faith as the Holy Spirit swept through that meeting! I remember not wanting to leave the service! Parents began to show up in the auditorium to see what was happening because no one was coming OUT at the normal time to head home!

Heading home that night in the back seat of the car, I was very quiet as I continued to sense that something had happened in my heart. *I was different.* I really KNEW that my life was going to be used by God and that He had just invited me to a MEASURE-LESS PLACE. It was a place I had never been to before, and all I knew was that I wanted to go back to that place over and over again! Everything in me wanted to know the power of God like I had experienced that night. Something had changed in me, and I knew it! Something also changed in what I believed about the life I could have in God! Ever since that moment in the seventh grade,

I've heard God repeatedly speak to my spirit, "I raised you up ⅟ this very purpose, that I might display my power in you and that my name might be proclaimed in all the earth" (Romans 9:17, NIV). In other words, "I have a work I would like to do through YOU so that many will come to know Me and there will be praise and honor brought to my name because of it!"

As God has given me more and more revelation on this thought through the seasons of my life, I've come to know and believe that I haven't been saved and been raised up to live in the predictable out of FEAR of the unknown! There have been moments where the devil has tried to dull that flame of hunger that started so many years ago in me to follow Jesus at a high level. He tries to put out any fire that moves us to action in God by setting before us the option of a "safe, quiet" life that no longer hungers to follow Jesus into the deep!

I realize that not everyone reading this book has had the same life experiences and that fear is very real when it comes to letting go and following Jesus. Do you remember that childhood game "Trust"? I have never liked that game, but it is a great picture of what I mean. You may remember how it goes: you stand in front of someone with your back to them and, without looking back, you are supposed to just willingly, trustingly fall into their waiting arms. The only problem is, most of the time, the "fun" is had by everyone else watching the person who is supposed to catch you step to the side, letting you fall! Everyone laughs at your awkward fall, and you learn that some people don't actually deserve your trust. (And that playing that game isn't worth the awkward fall!)

ral world, people fail us; they let us down, abuse us, and then throw us away. If that has been your sto- s to God. He wants to help you get through the painful ur history in order to bring you into the healing of your future. I realize it can be so hard to get past our own experience, but the name of Jesus is higher than even our own story so far. Down deep, you *want* to be able to stand in front of someone and, with your back to them and your eyes closed, fall back into their arms and have them actually be there to catch you. We all want that. Even if there is only a glimmer of hope in your heart for your life, that is more than enough for God to use to get you from where you are today and into His best plans for your life.

The Man and the Measuring Line

One of my favorite pictures the Bible paints is found in the book of Ezekiel. In this passage, God shows Ezekiel a vision of water coming out from the temple. A man measures the water using a measuring line as he leads Ezekiel forward into the water.

> As the man went eastward with a measuring line in his hand, he measured off a thousand cubits and then led me through water that was *ankle-deep*. He measured off another thousand cubits and led me through water that was *knee-deep*. He measured off another thousand and led me through water that was *up to the waist*. He measured off another thousand, but now it was *a river* that I could not cross, because the water had risen and was deep enough to swim in—a river that no one could cross.
>
> **Ezekiel 47:3–6 (NIV)**

I believe this small passage is significant because it exposes the issue of control. We like to know what to expect, how deep the water is, what kind of water it is, where it begins, and where it ends. But as the man continues to push forward with Ezekiel in tow, we see that they reach a place where the water could no longer be measured. This is the very place God is calling us to. I believe that God loves the MEASURELESS place. He loves it because it requires us to allow HIM to take us to the other side. As long as we can measure how deep and how wide the water is, to understand where the deep end is in order to keep a safe distance from it, we end up in control. We control what He is doing all the time, knowingly or unknowingly. And when we are in control, it doesn't require His presence for survival. We can save the day on our own! (Or so we like to think!)

This is the starting point for going deeper in God. The place where we surrender *our* ideas of what we think *we* need in order for us to serve God and follow Him. (And don't we just LOVE to tell Him our ideas!) If we require all the details before we launch out, we limit how far we can truly go in God. The truth is, we can always go deeper in God than we are right now. There is always MORE.

We can take great encouragement from those who have gone before us, as Hebrews 12 so beautifully points out! I believe that there are moments in heaven when the clouds are pulled back and the "great cloud of witnesses" looks on, cheering, as we "run the race marked out for us!" People like Abraham, who followed God into the deep to an unknown land and received the promise of a son. Or Rahab, a prostitute who was living in Jericho at the time the Israelites began to take the promised land and who risked everything in assisting God's people in capturing the city. The walls of Jericho literally collapsed all around her, and she was spared. Then there is Esther, who chose not to turn a blind eye to the injustice about to take place against the Hebrews but put her own life on the line and got involved to rescue an entire race of people. Or Peter. He focused on the voice of Jesus in the middle of the night in the midst of the sea during a storm and, against all logic, stepped out of the boat and walked on the water. Or the centurion who took Jesus at His word that His daughter would be healed, and she WAS! Hebrews 12:1–3 reads,

> Therefore, since we are surrounded by such a great cloud of witnesses, let us throw off everything that hinders and the sin that so easily entangles. And let us run with perseverance the race marked out for us, fixing our eyes on Jesus, the pioneer and perfecter of our faith. For the joy set before him he endured the cross, scorning its shame, and sat down at the right hand of the throne of God. Consider him who endured such opposition from sinners, so that you will not grow weary and lose heart.

Hebrews 12:1–3 (NIV)

All of these people and countless more are cheering us on from heaven as we run our own race. This is our time. But we first need to discover the measureless place.

The Secret Is Surrender

The secret to the measureless place is SURRENDER! There is no way to get into the deep and still have one foot planted firmly on the shore. Surrender is the only way to experience God's perfect plan for your life. It means giving over complete control. *Webster's Dictionary* defines "surrender" as the "relinquishing of possession or control of (something) to another because of demand or compulsion; to give up or give back." This is a significant and vital ingredient to living an effective and full life in God.

The moment we make Jesus Lord of our lives, we give Him possession of our lives. The beautiful thing about Jesus is that He doesn't take our lives out from under us. He waits for us to yield ourselves to Him! This is where the power lies. Not in Him taking of our lives but in our giving of our lives to Him. This is a deal breaker for many! We want *God* to have control and still be in control of our lives as long as *we* decide what areas and how much control He has. Right? We are happy to give Him control of those areas that really don't cost us anything.

As human beings, we aren't wired to surrender control. In the natural, we are wired to AVOID surrender, to do all we can to prevent losing control. But surrender is a spiritual principle. Wonderful things happen when we give over total control of our lives to Jesus—in every area. When we do this, we experience more freedom and joy than we have ever known before! It is the foundation that our faith is built upon. We bring ALL of our lives to Jesus, and He takes over. Jesus says, in Matthew 16:24 (NIV),

"Whoever wants to be my disciple must deny themselves and take up their cross and follow me." The moment this scripture becomes a reality in our lives is the moment we give up the right to call the shots and make the decisions. Jesus goes on to say in the next verse, "For whoever wants to save their life will lose it, but whoever loses their life for me will find it" (Matthew 16:25, NIV). Our biggest challenges in following Jesus into all that He has planned for our lives can usually be found in this area of surrender. God wants to take us to a place we've never been before in Him, but it WILL cost us. It will require sacrifice, and it will mean everything.

My mom and dad came to know Jesus right in the middle of the Jesus movement of the 1970s. They experienced Jesus in a real and powerful way and have followed Jesus faithfully ever since, which at the time of this writing, is over fifty years! I have watched my parents in good times and in difficult times. I have seen them fall to their knees in prayer during times when we didn't even know where our next meal was coming from, and I have seen them on their knees in worship during times of great blessing and prosperity.

I remember one time when I was young, and my dad had just been offered a great job that required our family to move from Virginia Beach to Chicago. A well-meaning friend came by our house as we were packing to move and asked my dad, "*How* are you doing this? It seems you *always* have to switch jobs and start over. Doesn't that just make you mad? I mean you are leaving your home for a place you don't know anything about! Isn't that hard?"

My dad looked at this sweet person and said, "You know what, it's actually okay because God gave me my 'job description' for life in 1972 when I gave my life to Him. He told me to seek first the KINGDOM and His righteousness, and all these things would be added to me! (Matthew 6:33) So, He can change my *assignment* as many times as He wants! My *calling* never changes. I can do whatever God asks of me and be fine as long as I am seeking Him above all else."

To this day, I have watched as my parents have faithfully followed Jesus into the deep. Into places of plenty and places of want, and no matter the season, Jesus has been there to meet them as they have learned to trust His voice.

A New Thing!

From The Message Bible, Isaiah 43:18–19 reads, "Forget about what's happened; don't keep going over old history. Be alert, be present. I'm about to do something brand-new." I believe one of the greatest gifts God gives us when we step into a measureless place in Him is new expectation! He creates in us a sense of anticipation about something that has yet to occur! One of the great benefits of salvation through Jesus Christ is a new hope. So many people have lost all hope for a good life because of multiplied disappointments and shattered dreams. These things can convince us that somehow it will hurt less to just have no expectations for our lives. Then when things don't happen or turn out the way we hoped, we won't have to be crushed by disappointment. This is one of the greatest robberies of the devil, the stealing of our hope!

Satan loves the idea of hopelessness and the suggestion of a dead-end with no way out.

Satan knows hopelessness because he is totally and completely without hope. There is no plan for redemption for him or for his fallen angels. But because of Jesus, *we* are never without hope, no matter what! Because of this, God wants to place within us a continual sense of anticipation about what He is able to do in our lives. This is a condition of our spirit that was designed to never "go away" over time! Our spirits are wired, by God, to stay on the edge of our seats in anticipation of what He's yet to do!

My husband, Paul, and I had been married about eight months when we started going to a new church in Birmingham, Alabama, where we were living at the time. We wanted to go to a "young couples" class so we could meet other couples our age and in the same stage of life that we were! I remember the first time we went. What a disappointment! When we walked into the class, the very first people we met asked how long we had been married. We proudly announced, "Eight months!" And one of the people standing near us joked and in a sarcastic and condescending way said, "Aw! That's cute; they still count in months! Just give 'em a couple of years" A few people laughed; I'm sure his wife felt "great" that he said this, and I was shocked and pretty deflated! I thought to myself, "Who put *THIS* shining beam of marital light in charge of 'encouraging' the young couples?"

Then I realized that somewhere along the way, something had happened, and this person had lost their expectation and anticipation for what God could do in a marriage and a family. Instead, he had become jaded, cynical, and hard when it came to the subject of marriage. Sadly, there was no LIFE and HOPE to transfer to a young couple (US) that day!

Expectation is what you BELIEVE about God and His ability! The devil tries to chip away at that expectation and undermine our anticipation of what God is able to do by causing us to live in our past. The devil knows we are defeated when we relive and rehearse the past, going over old history, as The Message Bible reads in Isaiah 43:17. God wants to fill our lives with His presence that always brings fresh grace, fresh power, fresh anointing, fresh vision, and fresh mission every single day! But if we cannot let go of what WAS, we can never go toward what is happening right now in God.

It is so critical to deal with the issue of "old history" before we set out to go to a deeper place in Jesus. It can be hard to let go of those things that weigh us down. But it is necessary! The "old history" Isaiah encourages us to forget is embedded in our memories and deep in our hearts. They are the events that have shaped us and try to define us. Have you ever noticed that our strongest memories are often of the worst events in our lives? You may not remember the family trips you went on as a child when the weather was clear and nothing bad happened. But you will never forget the time you went somewhere that was supposed to be a sunny paradise; instead, it rained for three days, and you were stuck in your hotel room. That's true for all of us, especially when those memories are traumatic. (We will talk more about this in later chapters!) But God's challenge is to let go of what is behind (in a healthy way) so that we will keep our eyes lifted as we look to the future and all that lies ahead!

Please hear my heart on this. If your "history" of pain or mistreatment and abuse was YESTERDAY or is fresh pain, this statement isn't for you right now. You need room to heal and deal with what happened before you are ready to let go of it. God understands where you are right now, and He will walk you through to the other side.

But concerning those of us who have ever gotten stuck as we have been "sitting" in our pain a little too long, chronically venting about it to anyone who will listen, Paul challenges us to shift and move forward in Philippians 3:13–14.

> Brothers and sisters, I do not consider myself yet to have taken hold of it. But one thing I do: Forgetting what is behind and straining toward what is ahead, I press on toward the goal to win the prize for which God has called me heavenward in Christ Jesus.

> **Philippians 3:13–14 (NIV)**

Our "old history" can be both good and bad! In the passage in Isaiah 43, as stated earlier, God tells the people through the prophet Isaiah that they will have to let go if they want access to the new thing He promises IS coming!

Anytime God challenges us to "let go" of something, it's not because He doesn't think what has happened to us doesn't matter.

Instead, God desires for us to be free; letting go is His way to bring us freedom and healing. The more we allow our minds to go over past hurts, offenses, and injustices, the harder it will be to believe and have expectation and anticipation that God will bring us into a new season of hope and healing. The same is true with past victories! We celebrate the answers to prayer and the faithfulness of God along the way, and we should! But if we endeavor to stay in that place permanently and build a monument to what was, we cannot be released into days of *new* victories and *new* promises God wants to bring us. Going over "old history" will keep our spirits stuck and dull instead of alert and present. It will prevent us from experiencing the incredible things God has in store for us and rob us of the on-the-edge-of-our-seats anticipation He desires us to have! Those places in our lives and hearts where we repeatedly rehearse the past are keeping us from being present in what God is doing TODAY. Allowing God to heal those areas, or even choosing just to be open to Him healing the broken places, is the best place to start as we head out into the deep.

Friends, this is the secret of the measureless place in God: to answer His call and give Him complete access to every area of our lives. He is still walking in the garden in the cool of the day and calling out your name! He is looking for you and longing to be with you. I can promise you that the measureless place is a wonderful place. And even though the water may be deep, Jesus will never leave you to drown. Jesus responds in such a powerful way when people dare to take Him at His word. He promises us His beautiful presence in Deuteronomy 33:26–27 (NIV), "There is no one like the God of Jeshurun, who rides across the heavens to help you, and on the clouds in his majesty. The eternal God is your refuge, and underneath are the everlasting arms." So, let's wade out a little deeper together. Come on in; let's go further!

LAUNCHING POINTS CHAPTER 1

- Is there an area of my life that I have been holding back from complete surrender to God because of a fear of losing control? Write down anything that God shows you, and then take the time to pray and invite God to completely take over every part of your life.

- Have I been holding on to my past experiences in a way that is keeping me from moving forward in God? Write down the areas of your life that God shows you. Take time to pray over any past experiences. There may be a person or people that you may need to forgive. Ask the Lord to help you.

CHAPTER 2

THE PROMPTING

One of the first and most important steps in moving into the measureless place is learning to hear the voice of God. That's right, hearing the voice of God! Take a look at Psalm 29:3–10.

> The *voice* of the Lord is upon the waters. The God of shining-greatness thunders. The Lord is over many waters. The *voice* of the Lord is powerful. The *voice* of the Lord is great. The *voice* of the Lord breaks the cedars. Yes, the Lord breaks in pieces the tall cedars of Lebanon. He makes Lebanon jump like a calf, and Sirion like a young wild bull. The *voice* of the Lord sends out lightning. The *voice* of the Lord shakes the desert. The Lord shakes the desert of Kadesh. The *voice* of the Lord makes the deer give birth, and tears away the leaves of the trees. And in His holy house everything says, "Honor to God!" The Lord sat as King over the flood. The Lord sits as King forever. The Lord gives strength to his people; the Lord blesses his people with peace.
>
> **Psalm 29:3–10 (NIV)**

Notice how many times the word "voice" is used in this passage. And consider whose voice is being described! It is such a powerful thing, the VOICE of God. Do you know that God is always speaking? It's true! He is speaking every moment of every day. And did you know that He is not just speaking to everyone else? He is also speaking to me and YOU! In fact, God says, *"Call to me and I will answer you and tell you great and unsearchable things you do not know"* (Jeremiah 33:3, NIV). Now, you may be thinking, "Why would God want to speak to me? And if He has spoken to me, how do I know if I have heard His voice? How does God speak?" Great questions! Let's take a look.

Hearing from God is something most people don't know they can do. Most people feel that there are some who can hear from God. Maybe a priest or a minister. Surely, *they* can hear from God. After all, it's their business to hear from God. Right? That's what they are supposed to do. Over the years, I have met with so many people who loved God and wanted to serve Him but never knew they could really hear God for themselves. It is possible to be saved and know Jesus yet never really have revelation on how to *hear* from God.

At times, I've been sitting across from people who, when asked the question, "Have you heard from God about that decision?" or "What do you think God is saying to you right now?" honestly admit they don't remember the last time they heard God speak to them! Crickets. Some have even admitted that they have never heard God speak to them! As you are reading these words, you may be thinking, "Hey, that's me!" I've got great news for you! It won't be you for long! God has plans for you, and every plan involves speaking directly to your heart. But, friends, if we don't learn how to hear from God and are satisfied with never developing our spiritual ears, we are in danger of heading down roads of unnecessary pain and making choices that were never part of His plan for us! Many of those roads and decisions cause regret, and that also isn't what God wants you to live in. He wants to give you direction, and He does want you to hear Him when He is sending you a warning! He's often warning all of us that we are maybe heading down a road that isn't His plan for us! Sometimes, He is sending a warning of physical danger! He also wants to speak words of life, hope, assurance, and peace to us. The question isn't, "Is God speaking?" But rather, "Am I listening?"

Why Would God Want to Speak to Me?

I want to tell you today that Jesus is Lord, Savior, and God, and most importantly, He is a very *personal* God. He cares *individually* about everything that concerns you and me, and He understands all that we go through. He calls us His own, His children and heirs. Because of this, He wants to speak to us. He wants us to learn how to hear His voice. In the same way that Adam could hear God's voice calling out to him as God walked along in the garden in the cool of the day, God wants us to hear His voice as He calls out to us, too. Only God does not want us to run and hide when He calls out our name as Adam did. He wants us to run to Him! The reason Jesus came to earth was so that He could walk OUR ROAD, so He would face the things we face. He didn't stand at a distance, but He was willing to come close and experience life the way we experience it and draw us to Him with His love. In fact, this is the motivation for God wanting to speak to you and to me: love. God wants us to turn to Him in every situation and hear His voice. It is so easy not to develop this area of our relationship with God, not to develop our ability to hear God. We get locked up in what we know, our denominational backgrounds, and ultimately our unbelief, and it stops us from hearing the powerful voice of God.

As I mentioned in the last chapter, there will be areas where you will be forced to re-evaluate what you really *believe* as you wade out into deeper water. You may have been raised in a very strict religious denomination where any aspects of a personal relationship were frowned upon. (God was "high," and you were "low," too low to think He cares about your daily life.) Or maybe you never set foot in a church until recently, or maybe never at all! And now you are being told that you can actually hear from God for yourself. Wading out into deeper water is going to require you to let go of some of the things you may have learned or assumed. Don't worry; you are not alone!

When we realize that *God* is reaching out to *us* and has made a way for us to bring whatever it is we are facing directly to Him, it is a powerful thing. Hebrews 4:16 (NIV) encourages and challenges us to "approach God's throne of grace *with confidence*, so that we may receive mercy and find grace to help us in our time of need." The confidence the Bible is speaking of here is the confidence of knowing who we are to Jesus. We are so important to Him! Because we are His children, His heirs of everything promised, we have direct authority and access! It's on this authority that we come to God.

It is important to address here that you understand that YOU have direct access to the presence of God if you have been saved and set free through Jesus Christ! ANYONE who calls on the name of Jesus is given access to the presence of God! This means you no longer need to go through a priest or a spiritual leader to have a relationship with Jesus! In his first letter, Timothy writes, "For there is one God and one mediator between God and mankind, the man Christ Jesus" (1 Timothy 2:5, NIV).

This is good news! We no longer need to go through anyone else to get to Jesus. When He died on the cross, He made a way. The work of the cross was to save us from our sins and to give us direct access to God. This means you can hear from God on your own! (This doesn't mean we forsake the guidance of our pastors or the messages we hear in church, or the need to BE in church.) It just means that you can hear from God on your own!

Because we serve a very personal God, we don't have to worry about how that will happen. Story after story in the Bible tells of the times when Jesus came to people in a way that they could understand! Consider the story in John 4, for example, when Jesus met the woman at the well and told her everything she ever did. Or the story in John 3, when Jesus met with Nicodemus, who came to Jesus at night so as not to be seen by others and explained to Nicodemus how to be born again. Or in Luke 24, when Jesus showed up on the road leading to the town called Emmaus to comfort people who were talking about His death on the cross and revealed His resurrection to them. Or in Acts 8:25, when Jesus prompted one of His disciples, Philip, by word of an angel to run on ahead and catch up to an Ethiopian man who was riding in a chariot. This man had been reading in the book of Isaiah and didn't understand what he was reading. Philip jumped up in the chariot and explained to the Ethiopian man all about the scriptures the man was struggling to understand. As a result, that man was saved and baptized into the name of the Lord Jesus Christ! These are just a few of the stories of Jesus meeting people where they were at the time and bringing them up to a higher level of understanding. I encourage you to go read some of the stories I've referenced above for yourself!

God wants to speak to you and to me in this same way. *He* comes to *us*! And He hears us when we come to Him! When God is truly speaking, you will find that anything He is saying to you will not contradict His Word. The Bible tells us that "God is not human, that he should lie, not a human being, that he should change his mind. Does he speak and then not act? Does he promise and not fulfill?" (Numbers 23:19, NIV). This is one of the greatest assurances we have as Christians—the assurance of God's Word!

The Voice of God—The Word

It is also important to understand that because Jesus wants to speak to us so clearly, the devil wants to block the TRUTH of His voice from our ears. So, he gets very good at imitating the voice of God, all the while attempting to distort the Word! He floats thoughts that might have a shred of what may sound like something God might have said, but it's not. The Word of God is where we learn to *discern* His voice from anything and everything that comes our way. We must learn to understand the very real power of the devil to counterfeit the authentic voice of God. We don't have to be afraid of the attacks of the enemy, but we most definitely must not be ignorant of his devices! (See 2 Corinthians 2:11.) How does the devil imitate the voice of God? Through lying spirits. They appear to be a legitimate authority but are not. Satan is the father of lies, the Bible tells us in John 8:44. This is all he knows how to do, lie and imitate! These counterfeit spirits come in many forms, including false prophets and preachers, spirit guides, psychics, clairvoyants/mediums (those that communicate with the dead), new age healers, horoscopes, shamans, gurus, etc. This is in no way an exhaustive list of how counterfeits will appear, but it gives you an idea!

As the people of God, we must learn to discern what is happening and never turn to these counterfeit voices to hear direction for our lives. In fact, it is vital that we actively reject any past associations with these practices. Jesus promised us, "I am *the* way and *the* truth and *the* life. No one comes to the Father except through me" (John 14:6, NIV). We don't need to seek wisdom and how to get our needs met from any source outside of Jesus and the Word. Jesus also calls Himself THE door, in John 10:8. (Notice He didn't say he was "A" door or one of MANY doors!) We can always discern if a voice is really from God or if it originated with a lying spirit by looking at what "door" into the spirit realm that voice is coming through. If someone is communicating with the dead, for instance, or telling fortunes, etc., the *door* they are using is dangerous because the Bible warns multiple times in both the Old and New Testaments to have NOTHING to do with people who engage in witchcraft! (And yes, this is witchcraft!) We are warned that this "door" is coming straight through Satan in order to *confuse* and *deceive* you into believing his lying wonders or miracles.

This is not a harmless association, nor is it a game. It is important that we become more aware of how *mainstream* witchcraft has become, even within people who are in the church, and will continue to be as the days go on! It is no longer just something happening in a dark room somewhere. It is right out in the open and masquerading as LIGHT. People may feel "encouraged" as they speak to their dead loved one through a medium, etc. This makes something that is dangerous seem safe! We are warned in 2 Corinthians 11:13–14 (AMP).

> For such men are counterfeit apostles, [spurious counterfeits], deceitful workers, masquerading as apostles [special messengers] of Christ [the Messiah]. And no wonder, since Satan himself masquerades as an angel of light. So it is not surprising if his servants also masquerade as servants of righteousness, but their end will correspond with their deeds.
>
> **2 Corinthians 11:13–14 (AMP)**

I know many people who have gone to see the latest "famous psychic or medium" in large settings like auditoriums and in one-on-one settings. It is a *thing*, as many of us know, to have a psychic at a party or a charity event to entertain people and give them "readings." It is often downplayed as "no big deal;" it's just for "fun"!

As we wade in a little more into this topic, it's important that we don't become *devil focused*! I view it as "devil aware" but JESUS FOCUSED! Remaining *ignorant* of the devil's devices is dangerous to us. Let me just say, don't "play" with the devil! The joke is never on him. Engaging in these things always comes with a price. If we *continually* dabble in any of these things, we open a door in our lives for a spirit of darkness to have access to us. We end up giving the devil *our* PERMISSION to mess with us!

I spoke with someone a few years back who was having horrific and very violent and graphic dreams. They were disturbing this person greatly and causing fear to overtake them! (To be clear, not every nightmare we have is like the one mentioned here. Every dream we have doesn't have a demonic element in it! Sometimes it really could be the spicy meal you had that night!)

This was different. The nature and intensity of the dreams caused something to stand up inside of me. As we continued to unpack the dreams more, the Holy Spirit led me to ask specific questions about any possible associations, past or present, this person had with anyone who operates in the "spirit" realm. Specifically in the form of the occult, or if there were objects that had come to my client through someone who believes a supernatural power can be stirred by and through that item. (Even if you think the object is just "pretty," the origin may not be!) I asked about what the client had been reading and what topics seemed to be predominantly attractive to them. I even asked about possible violent pornography. I also asked if they had been visiting a witchcraft store or buying items there. (This is way more common than you think!) As it turned out, *some* of these questions were answered with a yes. "Yes, I have done or am doing some of those things." And right there in front of us was the root of the violent nightmares!

This wonderful person wanted freedom and to get away from the darkness and paralyzing fear that had been welcomed into their home and life through their own participation. We prayed and watched God break those tight chains of torment off this person's life! He changed what had once been so desired! Every item connected with that way of life was thrown out completely. As growth has happened in the things of God alone, there is a new level of peace, and this is genuinely a different person now! Those nightmares have stopped completely and have not returned after the choice was made to shut that door and walk in the LIGHT.

When someone or something (a spirit, a voice, even an angel, etc.) comes through *Jesus*, and in *His* name, you know you can be open to what is happening because they acknowledge Jesus as the Source of what they are about to say! Especially when the focus is on the WORD of God and the wonder-working power of *Jesus*! There are many amazing prophets, preachers, teachers, pastors, evangelists, and everyday people who *are* using their voices to speak the TRUE Word of God. And God is moving through them greatly, even as we speak!

The voice of God can also come through visions, dreams, and words of knowledge. Acts 2 tells us that there will be an increase in the *way* God will pour out the Holy Spirit in the days to come! These are exciting times. Just make sure whatever it is that you are hearing points you to *Jesus* and gives all glory to Him alone. A word to the wise in ANY situation is to TEST everything that comes to you! Even with people you know who are speaking into your life. Hold up what someone or something is saying right up to the Word of God. (This means we better be IN the Word so that we know what it *really* says and be able to stand our ground!) If the two agree, you can become more open to receiving that voice! (Keep in mind that the Spirit and the Word always agree; they never contradict one another (John 16:13). Remember, don't get out of balance and start seeing devils behind every corner and bush! *Devil focused* is NOT our goal. Stay *Jesus focused,* and you will clearly recognize the counterfeit! Remember, the Bible clearly warns us,

> Beloved, do not believe every spirit [speaking through a self-proclaimed prophet]; instead test the spirits to see whether they are from God, because many false prophets and teachers have gone out into the world. By this you know and recognize the Spirit of God: every spirit that acknowledges and confesses [the fact] that Jesus Christ has [actually] come in the flesh [as a man] is from God [God is its Source]; and every spirit that does not confess Jesus [acknowledging that He has come in the flesh, but would deny any of the Son's true nature] is not of God; this is the spirit of the antichrist, which you have heard is coming, and is now already in the world.
>
> **1 John 4:1–3 (AMP)**

So how *does* God speak to us? First and foremost, as we are repeatedly establishing, He is speaking most clearly and most often through *His Word*. Psalm 119 says, "Your word is a lamp for my feet and, a light on my path" (Psalm 119:105, NIV). As we've already been encouraged, this should be the first place we run when we want to know what God is saying to us. Knowing the Word of God will help you make right decisions and experience God's peace in them.

I've worked for many years in church life as a pastor, and I've found that many people want to get answers and direction from spiritual leaders and look to *them* to be the voice of God in their lives. Friends, this is always a dangerous place to be! *People* should only confirm to you the things God has already been showing you! We are poor substitutes for the voice of God!

And just a quick note of caution here to those who are IN a position of spiritual authority: Beware of allowing anyone to place you in a position to be *the* voice of God to them. While it may be flattering to be sought after for your advice, it can actually slow down the spiritual growth of the other person! While simultaneously stirring the pride of your own heart into a dangerous place. Beware of this pattern in your own life! Instead, challenge those who come to you to ask God for direction; pray with them and for them to hear God's voice; offer godly council, but don't do the work for them. Allow *them* to press into God on their own for themselves. God wants their participation! Leave them dissatisfied with you in such a way that it causes them to seek out

His voice *over* your voice. God wants to strengthen and develop individual spiritual ears, and if pastors and leaders jump in too quickly, people will never look to Jesus for themselves. Raising up mature and strong believers requires strong, personal roots in God. No one can do this for you! Knowing and hearing God's voice is an ability and gift that God gives to all who call upon His name without reservation. It is His deep desire to have this kind of personal relationship with every one of us.

Baptism and the Fire

The way God amplifies His voice and gives razor-sharp direction and discernment, as we've already been speaking about, is through the Holy Spirit. Jesus said, speaking of the baptism of the Holy Spirit, "But very truly I tell you, it is for your *good* that I am going away. Unless I go away, the Advocate will not come to you; but if I go, I will send Him to you" (John 16:7, NIV). Jesus put incredible importance on the power of the Holy Spirit.

Stop and think about this for a minute. Why do you think there is so much resistance when it comes to the Holy Spirit among Christians? Why do you think various denominations argue over the outworking of the Holy Spirit within the church? It is so obvious when you consider all the ways the devil has tried to plant doubt about what the role of the Holy Spirit is for *today* deep inside the heart of many believers! Doubt that what happened at Pentecost is exactly what the Holy Spirit is *still* doing today. He (the Holy Spirit) never meant for that outpouring to STOP with the early church! Why is keeping the church of Jesus Christ quiet and contained so important to the devil? We just might use the POWER of the Holy Spirit to upset his agenda to spiritually stunt every Christian and take authority (*over* HIM)! It rattles him that we just might begin to move with boldness to change the world around us! We need to *hear* from God and *access* the power available to us to carry out what He is saying to us. And the truth is, this *same* power is just as accessible today as it was in the upper room to the disciples on the day of Pentecost!

One of my favorite evangelists is Reinhard Bonnke. He is now with Jesus in heaven, but through his ministry throughout Africa, according to Christ for all Nations (n.d.), well over 86 million documented souls came to know Jesus! His ministry lives on today and continues to burn brightly throughout the world. He once described the function of the Holy Spirit in his life as "power assistance." This thought resonated in me and brought me greater revelation on the Holy Spirit! This has become very true in my own life as well. I, too, look at what the Holy Spirit does in me as "power assistance."

I was seventeen when my parents bought me my first car. It was a "starter car," so it didn't have any real bells and whistles! It was an old Toyota Tercel. I first noticed something about it felt difficult as soon as I drove that car. It was so hard to steer! It had NO power steering! It was WORK to turn the car in any direction. I was thankful for that car, but when I got my next car, I was stunned by how EASY it was to drive and steer. It had POWER STEERING! I didn't know what I was missing out on or even how much work I had been doing to drive. The new car (a brand-new shiny black Ford Probe) had *power built in* to make what was so hard to do in an older car EASY to do!

When we receive the baptism of the Holy Spirit, we gain a heightened *enabling power*! He makes things that were once very hard to do (in our own strength), things like being BOLD and confident in even the quietest people among us, POSSIBLE! We gain a heightened sensitivity to the voice of God, a will to *listen* to conviction and obey Him, among many, many other wonderful things that become LOUDER within us! There is *more* of Jesus that is available to every single person who receives Him. Stay open as we unpack what this means. You don't want to miss out on this God-given power assistance for your life!

In Acts 2, something powerful happened. Take a minute and read it for yourself. There was a baptizing into the Holy Spirit—and fire! This is a separate event from salvation, evidenced through speaking in tongues. For more on this, read the book of Acts entirely. Notice the specific times when someone received salvation through Jesus, and the disciples told them of the gift of the Holy Spirit, something else happened! When the disciples laid their hands to pray for those who wanted this gift and promise of the Holy Spirit, they spoke in other tongues! This same promise, the baptism of the Holy Spirit and fire, is available to anyone who has accepted the Lord Jesus Christ as Savior. It was never meant to stop in the book of Acts! Acts 2:39 (NIV) tells us, "The promise [of the Holy Spirit] is for you and your children and for all who are far off—for all whom the Lord our God will call." It IS true that when you receive Jesus, you *are* receiving the Father, the Son, and the Holy Spirit. But the *baptism* of the Holy Spirit is different from what we receive with salvation! It is the step *beyond* salvation; it is a special and specific infilling given to equip each one of us by Jesus. Once you are saved, you are saved, and that is settled. (We aren't talking about salvation in this moment.) However, this *infilling* is yet to come to equip and empower you to walk with Jesus in great boldness. Given at your invitation to the Holy Spirit!

It is possible to *be* saved and in love with Jesus, yet never walk in the AUTHORITY Jesus died to bring you here on earth! The baptism of the Holy Spirit is something none of us were ever meant to live without. In the book of Acts, "Peter replied, 'Repent and be baptized, every one of you, in the name of Jesus Christ for the forgiveness of your sins. And you will receive the gift of the Holy Spirit'" (Acts 2:38, NIV). Notice what Peter just said. He said to repent and be baptized (in water), and you will receive the gift of the Holy Spirit. The only thing required to receive this infilling is that we have repented of our sins and given Jesus our lives! He was speaking of the progression that happens and culminates with the gift of the Holy Spirit. This is where the *power* lies.

If you notice in the account of the upper room, the disciples and others were hiding. Why? Because they were afraid. (Things were getting dangerous, and persecution was coming for them after the crucifixion and resurrection of Jesus.) And then, after hiding out for fifty days (that's where we get the term "Pentecost"—or "fifty"), the Holy Spirit swept through the room, and all who were present were baptized "in fire." Immediately afterward, they went out in boldness, no longer afraid, and preached the good news of Jesus. And many thousands of people were saved, and the church of Jesus Christ started exploding and spreading like wildfire, WITH FIRE! Jesus told them to WAIT and not to just start preaching. He knew they weren't ready for the assignment of "going into all the world" *without* the POWER of God! Jesus had no intention of sending the disciples, or anyone else for that matter, out into the world without the main tool for effectiveness! He knew they would need a supernatural infilling of the power of God to boldly proclaim the name of Jesus in the face of opposition, death, imprisonment, and torture! Jesus was readying them for the task ahead. And He is doing the same with people like you and me all over the world! He is readying US to fulfill the Great Commission with POWER!

Again, is it any wonder, then, that the devil is so opposed to people getting a greater revelation of the Holy Spirit? He takes great interest in keeping the people of God nice and quiet. He also takes great interest in keeping worship very quiet and subdued, restrained, and controlled so that nothing "weird" happens. Unfortunately, many streams of Christianity have been so afraid of what *might* happen if they let go of "the plan" and allow space for a real moving of the Holy Spirit to happen in a meeting that they have *quenched* the fire altogether! It's interesting how we wonder *why* miracles, signs, and wonders happen in the developing world on the regular and are so rare in the Western world.

One of the early American presidents, Thomas Jefferson, released his own "version" of the Bible, called "The Jeffersonian Bible." His version specifically and purposely removes and excludes EVERY one of the miracles of Jesus! (Go see for yourself!) He also made sure that *anything* was removed that spoke of the supernatural, including the RESURRECTION OF JESUS! (It denies the resurrection!) What we have in a "Bible" like that, or in a belief system that is uncomfortable with the work of the Holy Spirit, is simply an average book of RULES, with NO POWER to keep them! Nothing could be further from what God wants for each person all over the world! Unbelief and fear are two of the main reasons we only see signs and wonders rarely. Matthew speaks to this, referring to Jesus in His own hometown: "And they took offense at him…And he did not do many miracles there because of their lack of faith" (Matthew 13:57–58, NIV).

Unbelief and fear will always put LIMITS on what God will do in certain places! (Remember from chapter 1, we are going deeper to take the LIMITS OFF what God can do!) It's not because *He* is limited and CAN'T move. It's because He is not *welcome* to move. The Holy Spirit will never force His way! Instead, He will often wait to respond and fill an atmosphere where there is a genuine release of faith and freedom flowing. Since the Spirit and the Word always agree, we see this truth supported in 2 Corinthians, "Now the Lord is the Spirit, and where the Spirit of the Lord is, there is freedom" (2 Corinthians 3:17, NIV).

In this scripture above, this means there is freedom FROM sin and death, as well as freedom IN Jesus to access every promise He's made! In these very accelerated days, I believe God wants to move in GREATER power among His people. He wants to give you an open heart, a bold spirit, and a release of FREEDOM as He moves in you in unlimited ways! Maybe today is the day you ask God to come alive in you and fill you with the Holy Spirit! If you already ARE filled with the Holy Spirit, may I encourage you to ask for a FRESH infilling today? We can't live in yesterday's power. There is always more.

If you have yet to experience the power of God through the baptism of the Holy Spirit, simply follow what Acts 2:38 directs you to do: Repent of your sins, place Jesus as Lord of your life, and then ask for the Holy Spirit to fill your life. And He will! (See the prayer to receive the Holy Spirit at the end of this chapter.) As you unlock this area of your life through the baptism of the Holy Spirit, you will find that your spirit is much more sensitive to the voice of God. In fact, one of the main functions of the Holy Spirit is to reveal truth, to bring revelation! Consider what Jesus said about the Holy Spirit: "But when he, the Spirit of truth, comes, he will guide you into all the truth. He will not speak on his own; he will speak only what he hears, and he will tell you what is yet to come" (John 16:13, NIV). One of the roles of the Holy Spirit is to guide you—or lead you—into all truth as He reveals the Word.

The Holy Spirit will also change your appetite for God! You will find as you invite the Holy Spirit into your daily life and spend real time with Him that you will move from being satisfied with just a little of His presence and a "Sunday" relationship with Jesus to an insatiable hunger for the things of God! A hunger for God and His presence always brings a genuine move of God in our personal lives. It comes ALIVE in us! So much so that it overflows into the world around us. God responds to people who hunger for more of Him with "immeasurably more than all we ask or imagine, according to His *power* that is at work within us" (Ephesians 3:20, NIV).

In early 2012, my husband and I moved to New York City for an unexpected new season. We were part of a church during those brief years in the heart of the city. Every week, we witnessed thousands of people from all walks of life stream into whatever building we could find for that week's meeting in order to have an encounter with Jesus. New York City can be crazy at times because it is always changing, always moving; it is truly the "City That Never Sleeps"! Consequently, our church would gather in many different locations throughout the city each week! And on occasion, these locations would change—even on a moment's notice! Our greatest form of information sharing on venue and location changes would come using social media alone! (As it does in most churches today.) I never stopped being amazed at the way the people would just show up! By the thousands!

We would have church happening up and down Manhattan and lots of places in between, reaching people in the boroughs of New York and the surrounding states! And depending on the size of the venue, multiple services would be held in these places in order to accommodate all the people who show up each week. One week there would be two or three services. The following week, there may be seven or eight services because maybe the facility that week would be smaller. Somehow, it all worked! It was wild to me that people would move through all the last-minute changing locations and STILL show up! They would wait in line in all kinds of weather, sometimes for hours, to get into the house of God!

It was miraculous to see the outpouring of the Holy Spirit in response to the HUNGER of the people! People in that season were being saved and filled with the power of the Holy Spirit, baptized in fire as on the day of Pentecost. Hunger always brings the power of God. We are living in days where we all need ALL we can have of Jesus. We need the wisdom of heaven to know what our assignment is and the power of God to carry it out. Don't be fooled into thinking you can have the boldness you will need without the work of the Holy Spirit. Don't settle for the struggle when you can have THE POWER!

The Prompting

Another way God speaks is through the "prompting" of the Holy Spirit. What does that mean? A prompting usually comes in the form of a sudden thought that moves you to immediate action. I believe that if we develop our sensitivity to the voice of God, we will not miss His promptings as we venture out further and deeper in our relationship with Him.

When I was younger, I would be awakened at night. Often, I would lay there in my bed, trying to understand why I was suddenly stirred from my sleep. Then one night, I felt Jesus tell me to pray for one of my friends who was not saved and was in a very dangerous place in her life. I remember thinking at the time, "I might as well pray because I can't sleep." And so, I prayed. I prayed for quite a while, in fact. I remember praying for my friend, and as I prayed, I remember feeling even though I was praying for *her*, I was being drawn closer to God. As I entered my junior high and high school years, I continued to pray this way. I discovered that God was teaching me how to *respond* when He prompted me! As a result, in my adult life, I now recognize the prompting of the Holy Spirit, and I know it always involves action or a response on my part.

The promptings don't all come at night anymore! Because I have learned to respond to the Holy Spirit, I am prompted all the time and in various and different ways. For example, soon after my husband, Paul, and I moved to New York City, I was riding the train home after a Wednesday night service, alone. Not really knowing what I was doing yet or knowing my way around very well and not feeling very comfortable or safe as I sat there on the train alone, I was very preoccupied. Then, sitting further down the train from me, I inadvertently made eye contact with a woman. Then it came—the prompting. "Go and talk with her; she needs encouragement tonight. She's not doing well…Go!" I didn't get up right away, but I knew what I was supposed to do. Instead, I sat there in my seat and wrestled with it. "Is it even *safe* to do that, Lord?" I thought to myself. "I'm not sure it is. She looks pretty rough! And, besides, what am I going to say?"

THE PROMPTING

The prompting became so strong I could barely stand it. I knew what He wanted me to do, but my brain was frantically working to talk me out of it. I sat there for a few minutes, hoping this crazy idea of getting up from my seat, walking down the aisle of a speeding train, and starting a conversation with a perfect stranger would go away. But it didn't. So, I did the very thing my brain was telling me not to do. I got up from my seat and made my way through the center of the crowded train to where the woman was sitting and sat down next to her. As I began talking to her, she immediately responded and told me her whole story and everything she was going through. It was like she was bursting to open up to someone! I had the privilege of telling her how much Jesus loves her and that it was He who sent me to talk to her.

This woman, this perfect stranger, melted. I watched as the Holy Spirit began to minister to her. It turned out that she felt very rejected by the church and, as a result, felt that she was rejected by God as well over the course of her life. She felt that even if she *wanted* to come closer to Him or even try coming to church, her friends wouldn't be welcomed because of their lifestyles. I found myself saying things as if they were literally coming up from inside me. I was so excited to tell her that Jesus invites "WHOSOEVER WILL" to come to Him. And, that whosoever means everybody! That there is no "clean up" necessary before we ever become "good enough" to come! (Especially since that would disqualify every single one of us from coming to Jesus!) We are never *clean enough* on our own to come to Jesus; never forget that. To go even further, we can't wash *ourselves* from a sinful dead life; only

Jesus can do the washing. And we have to *come* to Him before that can happen! Just a thought here, but worth thinking about, *why* do we often require of people what Jesus never did? We can do better, church. I digress…

That day I was able, through the power of the Holy Spirit, to show her a glimpse of the heart of God that was toward her, drawing her in. It was incredible! I had yielded to the prompting and was able to participate with Holy Spirit as He went straight to the heart of this woman's need, with His love. He was speaking life to this woman, and He was building boldness and obedience in ME!

You see, my friends, promptings are usually not so much for us, nor are they always about us at all! These are the moments where God wants to USE us to bring HIM into a situation. These moments are also about obedience and willingness to be a messenger or an errand runner for Jesus. But we tend to make them more about us and what it might mean for us to obey! When we do, we end up missing the point entirely! We go right into self-focus thoughts like, "I'm scared!" or "It's not my personality to do that!" or "That would mean work for me; I have enough on my plate!" are common. But it is these types of thoughts that cause us to shrink back and become passive. The end result is NO action on our part. No partnering with heaven to see the perfect stranger; the rough-looking woman sitting on a train realized how insanely *LOVED* and *WANTED* she is by Jesus!

There are multitudes of people right now, like that woman on the train, who are in their own valleys of decision. They are hurting, and they need answers. Too often, we silence the promptings of the Holy Spirit and ignore Him. We can become indifferent to such a degree that it becomes a very real possibility that we might go through life and become completely deaf to the voice of God! Where we just stay consumed with our own lives. As a result, we miss all that God is doing in the supernatural realm. We miss going to the measureless places in God. The promptings of God to act on behalf of others is also His way of drawing us in deeper in Him. Elijah had an encounter with the voice of God in 1 Kings 19:11–13 that changed the way he listened.

> The Lord said, "Go out and stand on the mountain in the presence of the Lord, for the Lord is about to pass by."
>
> Then a great and powerful wind tore the mountains apart and shattered the rocks before the Lord, but the Lord was not in the wind. After the wind there was an earthquake, but the Lord was not in the earthquake. After the earthquake came a fire, but the Lord was not in the fire. And after the fire came a gentle whisper.
>
> **1 Kings 19:11–13 (NIV)**

What an incredible and powerful passage from the Bible! God is declaring that He is not always found in "showcase" moments but in the quieting of your soul, listening for His still, small voice.

A Soul at Rest

In order to hear the promptings of the Holy Spirit, we need a soul that knows how to REST in God! The kind of rest that I am speaking of here is not lying down and taking a nap! (Naps are pretty amazing, though!) The kind of rest that is essential for our souls is the kind that David speaks of in Psalm 62.

> Truly my soul finds rest in God; my salvation comes from him. Truly he is my rock and my salvation; he is my fortress, I will never be shaken… Yes, my soul, find rest in God; my hope comes from him. Truly he is my rock and my salvation; he is my fortress, I will not be shaken. My salvation and my honor depend on God, he is my mighty rock, my refuge. Trust in him at all times, you people; pour out your hearts to him, for God is our refuge.

Psalm 62:1–2, 5–8 (NIV)

David was speaking both *to* his soul and *about* his soul in this passage. He declares that his soul goes to a specific place to find rest, and THAT place is in the presence of God. Then he comes back around and speaks directly to his own soul and says, "Soul, since you find rest only in God alone, go there! Go back there again and find your rest in God alone!" A soul that knows how to rest or become quiet before God is one that will *hear* the voice of God. If we do not know how to wait *for* God and wait *on* God, then we can find ourselves in more of a "revolving door" type of relationship with Him, where we are just in and out and in and out and never quiet or "present" before Him long enough to hear from Him!

Our lives can be so filled with external noises and outside voices that "hearing" becomes impaired. We are so "connected" digitally that we have subsequently become *disconnected* from our SOURCE, Jesus. If our phone even looks like it's close to the battery dying, we are panicking to get to a charger as quickly as we can! It's interesting how unaware we are at looking at our own *spiritual* battery and responding accordingly! We just let it die before we even notice! We don't notice where the charge is on us! We should be saying things like, "Oh my gosh! My battery is really dying; I better get to the place where I can be recharged!"

The way things are today, and where they will continue to head, make us feel like it is almost impossible to ever shut down. To ever do what Jesus did and go away to a solitary place and rest awhile (Mark 6:31). Even Jesus realized that there was a lot of "battery" being drawn from Him and from His disciples! He recognized the need for solitude, to RECHARGE so that God could sustain them for MORE usability in the coming days.

I believe it is in THIS place of solitude and rest that we learn how to *practice* the PRESENCE of God. It is in this place that we can LISTEN and stop talking. (This is not a spa day, by the way, even though spa days are dreamy and are needed sometimes too!) These times are about YOU and JESUS. Connecting. You know you are being recharged as peace and focus start to come back, along with direction, vision, and strength! Sometimes there is a noise that can become deafening and threaten to block a soul at rest in us. This noise that many of us deal with regularly that can cause torment is nonstop *internal* noise. For example, we can be so preoccupied with our hectic schedules or problems that our minds and thoughts never shut off. Sometimes we can hardly sleep. I think we have ALL said things like, "I have got so much on my mind right now." Then there are times when our emotions are so overstimulated that any sort of downtime or stillness feels unproductive and unnerving! "I need to unwind, but I have so much to do!" With these internal "noise patterns" permeating our world and finding their way into our lives, it is no wonder that we struggle to hear the voice of God. When we understand that learning to wait on God, by learning to be still before Him, is crucial to hearing His voice above all the noises, only *then* we can begin to change the atmosphere of our lives and find rest. A soul that waits *for* God and waits *on* God is a soul that knows rest and peace.

I have found that God waits for us to get quiet before Him, and *then* He speaks. We tend to operate with God in a rush and on our terms and timetable. We want His answers to follow that same pattern and "rush" right back to us. But I believe God wants us to train our souls to do as Psalm 37:7 (NIV) says, "Be still before the Lord and wait patiently for Him." There is an element of waiting and listening that gives God the *room* to speak clearly to us. It also gives *us* room to receive from Him. Sometimes I wonder if, when we eventually do get quiet and calm down, He sighs and says, "FINALLY! NOW I can speak to you!" This is the clarity with which God is able to speak or give us direction. The Holy Spirit's leadership is what so many of us want but lack. We lack this clarity because we haven't waited long enough in the presence of God to hear what He has to say. We miss out on the peace and confidence that comes from being close to Him.

Our modern-day culture has created much of this rush and immediacy, particularly here in our part of the world! We live in such a technical world with so many amazing conveniences. We are hardly forced to wait for anything today! In fact, we are even personally insulted at times when we are told there is a *wait*. We won't consider going back to a restaurant that "took too long," or seeing a doctor who leaves us in the waiting room "too long," or we become incensed when our friend doesn't immediately text back! Sitting down and actually writing a letter has been traded for a quick tweet, text, or DM. Family photos that used to be sent through the mail and shared around the table are now mostly seen through any of the social media outlets! (These things aren't all bad!) And then there is sitting in traffic! I'm pretty sure we are all on the same page there!

In short, we have become so accustomed to the immediacy of our modern world. The idea of "instant" has literally transformed the way we think and act. Most of us, if we are being honest with ourselves, do not like to wait for anything. We are so used to having virtually anything we want when we want it. Same-day service, same-hour service, delivered to our door! (Which, let's face it, is pretty great!) The danger is that we can turn our *faith* into some sort of fast-food meal. If we aren't careful, we can literally approach a church service on Sunday morning in this same way! To give you a picture, we pull up to the church, hoping for a "drive-through" service! We pull off the road, running late ourselves, yet still annoyed that the kid's team is backed up. Entitled as we are, we want to squeeze to the front of that line and get our kid situated first, make sure everyone knows that THIS team "needs work," we head into the auditorium, get to our seats and pray with all our might the preacher isn't long winded today and that the worship team will play our preferred set list favorites! Then we can't figure out *why* we aren't feeling "fed" spiritually as we try to live on that one badly digested, very cheap spiritual "meal" for the week until the next Sunday service! (And we wonder why we aren't hearing from God and living in victory!)

Someone who has trained their soul to listen for and hear the still, small voice of the Lord is one who has learned how to cultivate the presence of God in their *everyday* life. To get direction for our lives, we must have real time set aside every day with Jesus. Time when we read His Word, time when we pray in the Spirit and with understanding (1 Corinthians 14:15), and time to LISTEN for His voice. The key word here is "time"!

We cannot allow ourselves to become lazy in this area if we want to go "into the deep" in our relationship with God. There are no shortcuts when it comes to knowing Jesus. You can't know Him through another person. In other words, many times, we turn to people to get advice or their "perspective" on our lives. There have been many times in my own life where I have done this and felt the whisper of the Holy Spirit say to me, "Actually, I haven't spoken to *them* about *you*. I'm speaking to YOU about YOU!" Understand the balance here, I am not saying that we should never seek out good and godly counsel, but as we have already established, we need to be careful that we are not substituting human wisdom for the voice of God in our lives!

When God is calling us "into the deep," He is lovingly inviting us into a deeper and stronger relationship with *Him.* It's out of this authentic relationship with Jesus that we are brought up higher and able to go out further into His great plans for our lives! Like any relationship, it takes time spent with the other person while learning to recognize their voice and personality. This is especially true as it concerns our relationship with Jesus. It's getting a little deeper. Don't turn back now!

LAUNCHING POINTS CHAPTER 2

PRAYER TO RECEIVE THE BAPTISM OF THE HOLY SPIRIT

Lord Jesus, I thank You for the gift of the Holy Spirit. I thank You that through the work of the Holy Spirit, You will reveal who You are to me in a greater way. Lord, I don't want to just know about Your power and all You have for me; I want to walk in this power. I want to experience that same power that raised You, Jesus, from the dead. I want this filling of the Holy Spirit to be part of my every day. I ask You, Jesus, to fill me right now with the baptism of the Holy Spirit. I welcome You, and I want all that You have for me. I receive this gift of the Holy Spirit, and I pray this in the name of Jesus. Amen.

NOW, LET'S TAKE THE NEXT STEP

After you have prayed this prayer, it is important that you begin to praise God for filling you with the Holy Spirit! You don't have to keep begging! When you praise God, it shows that you believe His Word. You praise Him because you know and believe that He has done what you have asked of Him! As you thank Him and praise Him in your own language for a few minutes, then shift and begin to speak in tongues. If you have asked Jesus to fill you, then you are filled, so begin to speak out whatever begins to come out of your mouth, whatever those sounds may be.

Keep in mind that *you participate* in this moment! *Just pray, "Jesus, I give You my tongue."* Then begin to make sounds as you, in FAITH, surrender your tongue to Him. You will sense that the Holy Spirit is moving within you as you focus on Jesus while you are worshiping Him and beginning to move your mouth in new ways. The more you speak in tongues, the bolder and more confident you will become in the language that God gives you. Also, keep in mind that there is no "right way" to speak in tongues! What comes out of YOU might be totally different from what comes out of someone else. So don't compare and feel that you aren't "doing it right." Go with what the Holy Spirit is giving *you*! And USE IT. Keep praying in this way as much as you can. Let God stir up the gift of the Holy Spirit and strengthen it within you!

One common misconception about the baptism of the Holy Spirit is that you have no control over what comes out of your mouth! God is a God of order and gives us rule over our own spirit. We actively and consciously decide to begin to pray in the Spirit and operate in this gift. The Holy Spirit does not "possess" us. He fills us! So be *filled,* in Jesus' name!

TWO COMMON LIES

There are two common lies the devil uses on anyone who has just prayed to be filled with the Holy Spirit! I feel compelled to warn you of them so that when he tries to use them on you, you can shut them down immediately!

> **Lie #1:** You are making this up! The words and sounds coming out of your mouth cannot be real. This is fake.
>
> **Lie #2:** You might have prayed in tongues once, but you will never be able to do it again! This was just a result of being caught up in the moment. And now the moment is over.

These are lies because we know from the Word of God that we can ask God anything that is in line with His Word, and we know that He has heard us. First John 5 tells us, "This is the confidence we have in approaching God: that if we ask anything according to his will, he hears us. And if we know that he hears us—whatever we ask—we know that we have what we have asked of him" (1 John 5:14–15, NIV). As you pray to be filled with the Holy Spirit, concentrate on this scripture from 1 John and allow faith to fill your heart and spirit as you step out into this new season marked by the desire for MORE of God!

CHAPTER 3

UNWAVERING TRUST

God wants to take us out further than we've ever been before, but we will have to learn how to trust His love for us and allow Him access to our lives. Our whole lives. Every area. We have to give Him permission to peel back the layers of who we really are—the person we are when we are all alone and no one is looking. The real us. And for many, this is not easy. Why? Because down deep, many of us don't trust God. What we don't often realize is that trusting God is never a finished work! We will always be a student learning how to trust Him more and more. This seems to be especially true when what God is asking you to trust Him with seems fragile and hard to release to Him. There is one thing you must know as you read this chapter is that wherever you are on your journey with God, you can trust God! He loves you, and He never condemns you or is mad at you, especially for moments of doubt or unbelief. Read what David wrote about God: "Hear my cry, O God; listen to my prayer. From the ends of the earth I call to you, I call as my heart grows faint; lead me to the rock that is higher than I. For you have been my refuge, a strong tower against the foe" (Psalm 61:1–3, NIV).

God simply wants you to have a greater understanding of who He is so that when the storms come, you will cling to Him and trust that He will carry you. David understood this. He also knew the reality of his own human heart. That it grows faint. That it becomes overwhelmed. That it fails. That there would be many things that would be impossible for David to carry. He knew God as a refuge and a strong tower. He reminds his soul over and over again throughout the book of Psalms of how to get through the rough places. David was willing to put his trust in God.

Fear Is Not Faith

Looking honestly at the journey of my own life, without a doubt, my greatest challenge in the area of trusting God has been and, being honest, is still overcoming worry and fear! It started when I was very young. I remember the first time I experienced fear and dread. I was in the second grade, and my best friend had a little brother just like I did. We didn't just love our little brothers! We adored them. They were both spoiled rotten because of all the love we all gave them. One afternoon, as my best friend and her little brother were playing in the backyard, her little brother ran out of the backyard and chased a ball into the street. He was hit by a passing car and died instantly. He was only three years old at the time.

I remember hearing the news of the tragedy. I was profoundly affected by what had happened. And the devil seized upon this opportunity to plant seeds of paralyzing fear into my life. Those seeds sank deep into the fabric of my life. As I grew older, I became known to everyone in my family as the "caregiver." But it wasn't because I had a deep sense of care so much as I had a deep sense of *fear,* and this is what was motivating me! I was afraid of losing someone precious to me. So, I threw myself into looking out for everyone. (A codependent was developing inside of me in the worst way!) It was exhausting! I literally wore myself out at times as I tried to *manage* everyone for whom I cared so deeply in order to control my fear of losing them.

I worried when my mom wasn't right there to pick me up after school ("What if she was in an accident? What would I do?"). I worried when my dad was on a business trip ("What if the plane goes down and I never see him again?"). In fact, there was a period when my dad traveled extensively, including frequent trips to the warzone of Beirut, Lebanon. I feared he would be killed or kidnapped. I just about went out of my mind, allowing every possible scenario to send me into a tailspin! There was a constant torment. I worried about my sisters and that something horrible would happen to them or that they would die in some way. And then there was my brother! I worried about my brother all the time, traumatized from my friend's little brother's death. I worried he would drown in the pool or fall down the stairs or get lost at the mall when we went shopping. I was gripped with fear and torment, and the fear was unwavering!

Then over the years, fear and worry would try to go to new levels, especially after I got married and later as I entered ministry. After I was newly married, I was hardly home from my honeymoon and already worried that the "honeymoon" would be over and my husband would lose interest in me. I had already begun to visualize a "ships passing in the night" existence, and nothing like that was an actual reality! It was fear. In ministry, I worried so much about failing. I took my role of pastor so seriously, and frankly, too seriously, that the lines would become blurred at times. I felt that if my pastor, to whom I reported, wasn't happy with my performance in some way, then perhaps God wasn't happy with what I was doing either! I worried about not being good enough or qualified enough; I was a generalized worrier! My fear and constant worry brought on insecurity and doubt. The good news is God was always there. Even when I didn't recognize His presence or He seemed a million miles away, He was still there. He was (and is) always watching. The following is what David said of the Lord in Psalm 139:

> Where can I go from your Spirit? Where can I flee from your presence? If I go up to the heavens, you are there; if I make my bed in the depths, you are there. If I rise on the wings of the dawn, if I settle on the far side of the sea, even there your hand will guide me, your right hand will hold me fast.

Psalm 139:7–10 (NIV)

David learned and then constantly reminded himself that God was always with him. He discovered that God was with Him in every battle he fought or the times he fled for his life and ended up alone in a cave. God was there. In the same way, I have also discovered that God was—and is still—watching over me. As I grew and matured, God would continually bring things to the surface in my life in order to set me free from them. (And He continues this work in me today!) He wants to do this same work in you! We all have things that try to pull us down, to destroy us, to cause us to shrink away from God. But when I began to trust God, He began to set me free so that I could go deeper in Him. I no longer had to live in such a tormenting state internally. It is never God's will for us to be tormented by fear and unbelief. I began to prevail against the fear so deeply embedded in my life. And with every battle I have fought and won in this area of my life, God would build and strengthen within me a deeper and unwavering TRUST in Him.

Every Battle Matters!

Maybe as you read this chapter, you have worries concerning your finances, or your children or your marriage, or maybe concerning your health. Maybe you have questions about things that have happened in your life that you don't understand, and these things leave you in a very legitimate place filled with doubt and unbelief as it concerns the goodness and faithfulness of God. It is important to say here that there aren't solid answers and reasons made known to us on earth for everything we have gone through. We want to know *why,* we want to know *if* things will change, and we want to know *how* God plans to set that record straight and bring justice to your cause! I believe that even in this moment, as you bring each place of fear with all your questions to Jesus, He will bring peace and assurance of His presence into your life. He wants to do this so that you can experience the release of those knotted places and pieces of your heart. All the while giving you special grace as you begin to TRUST Him more.

It is virtually impossible to move into a deeper relationship with God and live in fear, worry, doubt, and insecurity. We cannot allow these things to be a permanent fixture in our lives if we really want to experience God's victory in us, causing His power to flow through us! I want to say, however, that there is NO condemnation over your life if this is an ongoing battle. (Join the club!) Jesus will help us every step of the way. He will show us Himself, proving over and over that He is true to His word and can be trusted.

There is a great plan and purpose of God for every person who believes in the Lord Jesus Christ. The Bible promises this! Jeremiah 29:11 tells us that God has GOOD plans for us, and they are full of HOPE and the promise of a FUTURE! However, we must face the evil plan of the devil to shrink our expectation of God through fear. We must face the evil plan that would shroud God's goodness in doubt and cause us to resist taking God at His Word.

Whether you have known Jesus for one hour or for decades, this issue of TRUST will always be at the forefront of the work of God in our lives. Let me state that again. The issue of TRUST will always be at the forefront of the work of God in our lives. Stated another way, TRUST is a critical component of our relationship with God. If we don't learn how to truly release the things that are holding us back, or even the things we hold dear, even our hopes and dreams, continually back into the hands of God and trust them to His care, we literally limit our ability to be used of Him at the level to which we are actually called.

Trust and Faith in Trials

Trust is the beginning of true FAITH. FAITH says, "I can believe You, God, in this circumstance I am facing because I TRUST you!" God wants to give us MORE faith over fear and MORE belief over unbelief because of how much He loves us. Faith fans into flame what we truly believe about God. Fear fans into flame everything we *don't* believe about God! As a result, we hold tightly to all that we have yet to give over to Him! It's in the trials that we find out how much of everything we have learned and read and written about God is truly alive and working in our lives.

I get a sense, even as I write these words, that there are some reading who may feel immediately condemned with failure inside because of the level of fear that is permeating them right now. Please know that there is NO shame in dealing with fear as you are learning how to move more in faith. We are ALL on this constant journey with you. What we are talking about in this moment is the TRUTH of where God wants us to go with Him. But NO ONE is fully there. I, for one, am not fully there! God is working on each one of us daily when it comes to fear and faith. As soon as you get through one faith moment, you can be sure God is strengthening you for the next time of believing Him.

It's not easy to trust God when it seems like our world is falling apart. When the layoff comes, and the ends don't look like they will ever meet, or when the diagnosis comes and the prognosis is grim, or when infertility disappoints an aching heart month after month as others celebrate the birth of their new babies, or when a child walks away from everything they have been taught, or when a marriage is failing and everything seems to be spiraling out of control; these are the times when it is most difficult to trust God.

If you are facing a trial right now, let me encourage you: Jesus is standing WITH you, and His heart is toward you. The Bible declares in Psalm 34 that "the Lord is close to the brokenhearted and saves those who are crushed in spirit" (Psalm 34:18, NIV). As you desire to follow Jesus "into the deep" even through the storms, you will find Him to be faithful.

Trust doesn't deny the existence of a need! It simply shifts our focus from what we *see* to what we *know* God is ABLE to do! No situation is ever too dark for Jesus to illuminate, no situation too big for Him to handle. He can step in and, in a moment, change it all. Jesus said in John 16:33 (NIV), "I have told you these things, so that in me you may have peace. In this world you will have trouble. But take heart! I have overcome the world." So, take heart! God isn't finished yet!

Worship

You might be asking, "How can I take heart when all seems lost?" God gives us many weapons we can use in the heat of battle! However, none of the weapons God uses to give us the victory are *natural* (or man-made). They aren't what the world would ever think could cause a nuclear explosion in the kingdom of darkness! (See 2 Corinthians 10:4 for what the Bible says to fight with!) In my life and journey, I have found that one of the most powerful weapons to wield when the enemy is raging is the power of WOR-SHIP. Bringing praise and worship into our lives when we are in a fight to trust God silences the enemy's voice of doubt! This is why it is such a powerful weapon. God never leaves us powerless and without resources to come against the devil's attempts of destruction in our lives. I know that may sound crazy, but it is true. "God has ascended amid shouts of joy, the Lord amid the sounding of trumpets," David declared in Psalm 47:5 (NIV). The King James Version reads, "God is gone up with a shout, the Lord with the sound of a trumpet." I love that! God begins to move on our behalf when we begin to praise Him. It is through our worship and praise of Jesus that we develop an *overcoming* spirit. It is a place where we choose to position our souls. It is a STANCE we choose to take in battle! Nothing shifts our attention off the panic of our immediate need more than reminding our soul WHO our God IS! Again, look at another psalm David wrote as it concerns the power of praise. Psalm 34 is so powerful because in it we see David speaking to his own soul.

> I *will* bless the Lord at all times: his praise *shall* continually be in my mouth. My soul *shall* make her boast in the Lord: the humble *shall* hear thereof, and be glad. O magnify the Lord with me, and let us exalt his name together. I sought the Lord, and he heard me, and delivered me from all my fears.

> **Psalm 34:1–4 (KJV)**

Worship is giving God the highest place, and because of this, worship REPOSITIONS our circumstance or situation well BE-

NEATH the feet of Jesus. Reminding us that whatever is happening, even in the most impossible of circumstances, is NOT bigger than Jesus. By worshipping God, we stir up FAITH that allows Him to take the highest place in our mind and heart. It will also help give us supernatural PEACE right in the middle of the storm. Our spirit becomes encouraged, and we become empowered by God to deal with our circumstances. The bigger God becomes on the inside, the smaller our circumstances become. David's words in Psalm 34 should remind us that God is in control and that He sits high above it all. And when His presence comes, He delivers us from all fear.

This is what I like to call a "supernatural exchange." Worship is the place where we trade the brokenness of our lives in exchange for the peace and power that God's presence brings. We cannot declare how great our God is and, at the same time, hold on to our unbelief, worry, fear, and doubt. If we struggle with any of these areas, our praise and worship bring Jesus onto the scene in a way that silences the enemy. He brings relief from the exhaustion of trying to figure it all out and fills us with His promise instead. But we have to participate by releasing all that weighs us down, exchanging it in order to experience peace. When you declare who God *is* and worship Him, even in the midst of dark times, something happens! Faith rises, and hope returns to your spirit again. Isaiah 61:1–3 shows us how this "worship exchange" happens.

> The Spirit of the Sovereign Lord is on me, because
> the Lord has anointed me to proclaim good news to
> the poor. He has sent me to bind up the brokenheart-

ed, to proclaim freedom for the captives and release from darkness for the prisoners, to proclaim the year of the Lord's favor and the day of vengeance of our God, to comfort all who mourn, and provide for those who grieve in Zion—to bestow on them a crown of beauty instead of ashes, the oil of joy instead of mourning, and a garment of praise instead of a spirit of despair.

Isaiah 61:1–3 (NIV)

Worship is the place where this supernatural exchange happens! This is the place where our belief in Jesus and who He really is is strengthened. In this place of worship, our ability to TRUST God apart from what we SEE with our eyes begins to soar, and what comes next is the best part—VICTORY! Something incredible happens in the spirit realm when we choose to bring the power of praise into a situation that otherwise would weigh us down or try to destroy us! It happened to Paul and Silas when they were imprisoned.

Paul and Silas had recently left the town of Troas and made their way to the town of Philippi in the region of Macedonia. While there, they preached the gospel, and many people were saved, including a wealthy woman named Lydia and her entire household (see Acts 16:11–15). They continued to preach in the city, all the while followed by a young woman who was possessed by a demon. She followed and harassed Paul and Silas for a number of days until Paul, irritated and frustrated, couldn't take it any longer. The account in Acts 16 says he turned around and cast the demon out of the young girl (verse 18). This moment caused a massive scandal in the town. Paul and Silas were subsequently arrested, beaten, tied down in chains, and then thrown into the inner or deepest part of the prison (verses 19–24). Nothing about this experience in the natural was praise-worthy. Yet in the darkest moment, when all hope seemed lost, Paul and Silas remembered Jesus and ignited the power of praise! They remembered that even though their bodies were chained, it was impossible to imprison and chain the power of Jesus Christ! So, they began to SING. Read what happened next.

> About midnight Paul and Silas were praying and singing hymns to God, and the other prisoners were listening to them. Suddenly there was such a violent earthquake that the foundations of the prison were shaken. At once all the prison doors flew open, and everyone's chains came loose.

Acts 16:25–26 (NIV)

If we are being honest, we know that there have been times in each of our lives when we have faced some incredible difficulty; you may be facing a difficult situation right now. And the last thing to do that seems reasonable is to worship. Right? We seem to be more inclined to sit in worry and fear or maybe even withdraw from the presence of God. Sometimes the heat of the battle is so high that you go silent, out of trauma, disillusionment, disappointment, betrayal, shock, sickness, and the list goes on! When we can't get our bearings, we feel weakened and just want to physically sit down or even crawl under the covers to get away from the pain. I have been at this point myself many times. I know personally how hard it is to find your song on days like this.

Stay Home

Have you ever noticed when you are in the midst of a fire that you begin to think thoughts like, "Stay home from church this week; you need some time to yourself"? There are times when this may really be the case for many reasons. There is no shame in needing a "minute" to gather yourself. It's okay to breathe if that is what you need to do from time to time. But the devil has this way of turning "time to time" to "every time" I am in a battle, I stay HOME. He tries his absolute best to keep us away from those places that will help us get a breakthrough in our spirits—and our situation. And honestly, there have been times when I have listened (sadly) to the devil's rationale and stayed home past the point when I really should have returned!

The devil wants you anywhere but in the presence of God when you are in a battle. Why? Because when you run to the house of God and gather with other believers, you gain the courage to keep believing God and His Word for yourself! In the passage in Acts 16, it says that the prisoners were *listening* to Paul and Silas as they worshiped. Their worship even set the prisoners around them FREE!

You may be in the trial of a lifetime right now, but the breakthrough God wants to bring into your life isn't just for you! Yes, He wants to see you set free. But your worship can unchain other people around you too. Praise God for the overflow! But, my friend, don't wait for the next church service to worship Jesus. Start singing right now, right where you are! Sing! It's not about whether you are a singer or not! It doesn't matter if you are musical or not or if you are outgoing or an introvert! None of that matters. What does matter is that you start to worship the Lord right where you are, right in the midst of your circumstances. Worship isn't about me and my situation; it goes way ABOVE all circumstances. It's about how worthy Jesus is. In Psalm 137, the author (the author of this Psalm is unknown) describes what it was like to be an exile in captivity in Babylon as he writes,

> By the rivers of Babylon we sat and wept when we remembered Zion. There on the poplars we hung our harps, for there our captors asked us for songs, our tormentors demanded songs of joy; they said, "Sing us one of the songs of Zion!" How can we sing the songs of the Lord while in a foreign land?

Psalm 137:1–4 (NIV)

Too many times, we find ourselves in a "captive land" because of the circumstances in our lives and hanging up our harps! Stated another way, we hang up our praise! The children of Israel were famous for their praise! But because of their grief and sadness, they stopped singing!

Harps aren't meant to hang on trees! They are meant to be played! Your praise wasn't meant to stop when the trials came. Even if the words feel hollow in the moment as you begin to sing IN the pain. But what starts out as sometimes an empty start with hardly any sound, let alone *feeling*, turns into a supernatural moment! God always meets us in these most intense moments, and He supplies the grace and relief we are so desperate for. He changes the atmosphere of our hearts! That change overflows into the room and then into your faith level. You start to BELIEVE He is who He says He is, and He can do what He says He can do!

My journey has had its share of challenges and has taken me places I never imagined. About twenty years ago, my husband and I had decided we wanted to start a family. We had already been married five years at the time we were now ready. After almost a year of nothing happening, we began to seek out answers for why we weren't getting pregnant. I ended up in the office of one of the top fertility doctors on the East Coast, and many tests and thousands of dollars later, I was told my situation didn't look promising. She said that if I was compelled to continue, my "window of opportunity" was less than two years and was closing. After that time, she told me that there would be virtually nothing they could do for me. I was speechless as I sat in my chair across from this fertility specialist. I was still in my twenties! I was healthy and vibrant! And as I sat there in the office, I attempted to process everything I was hearing. I could hardly wrap my head around the medical report. Then it suddenly occurred to me: this news is becoming my story, my new reality.

I remember sitting in that doctor's office that afternoon as wave after wave of emotion flooded over me: shock, disbelief, anger (definitely anger), disillusionment, injustice, anxiety, sorrow, all of it! It didn't make sense. I mean, after all, isn't it okay to want children? I remember asking myself, "What if it never happens? What if I can never have children?" and "How does my husband feel about me now? Does he still love me?" These thoughts tormented me as they raged through my mind!

Sing!

My thoughts were in danger of leading me down a path that would drown me. And I tell you the truth; God stepped in. He said, "Sing!" Sing when you don't have the answers. Sing when you don't understand. Sing when your heart seems irreparably broken. SING!

Now, twenty years later, I sit in a place that is so full of the life of God because Jesus really does *fill* every broken place. There are things on this side of heaven for which we believe God that we may or may not see happen. And we may never understand why. We may never get the answers that explain everything we want to know. But God is faithful…and He is good. When God saw me in my despair and spoke into my heart, telling me to sing, I had to *decide* in that moment that my praise would have nothing to do with whether God would EVER give me what I was believing Him for or give me an explanation for all the things that I don't understand! That was a "line in the sand" moment for me. I knew God was asking me to release it all to Him. To clarify, this wasn't easy. I struggled, wondering if "release" meant "giving up." I sensed God give me peace as He put inside of my heart that releasing something I wanted so badly to Him was about to give me FREEDOM. Giving up means you no longer have hope. Releasing means that I am placing ALL my hope in the God who can do anything about everything! It means my hope is *still* active! It rested then, and it rests still in *Jesus*, who stays the same yesterday, today, and forever. My hope was no longer in MY plan, MY way. He had my surrender to move the way He chooses! *That* was the day my praise became my LIFELINE. My praise is about WHO JESUS IS! And my praise is still my lifeline.

Unwavering Trust with All My Dreams and Desires

Over the years that I served in church life as a worship pastor, I encountered many skilled and capable people. I discovered that some of these people were very much attached to their "gift" and "calling." While we are all called and gifted by God to be effective on this earth, we are not called to place our gifting or calling or identity possessively in a "box"! Restricting God's ability to use us TO that box and that box alone! When we do this, we are deciding that He can only use us in one way (our way) and become rigid with what we *will* do for God!

It is not uncommon for any of us to decide *how* we are going to use the gifts and talents we have. (We think we know so much! Ha!) We have the right to *try* to control our lives and destiny, and God also reserves the right to throw that tightly controlled plan right out the window! (I bet He is amused at our attempts to write our own course.) I don't know about you, but I don't want the contained version of the life God has planned for me! I've seen this become a stumbling point for many gifted and talented musicians or singers, even many pastors and leaders who have not learned how to trust God with the gift, talent, and calling He has given them.

Trusting God to make the way and to do it in His timing is something every person must learn on the journey of life with God. It can be so easy when it comes to gifts and talents and goals and dreams to forget that IT ALL belongs to God! He created us with special gifts and abilities for purposes He had in mind. He fills our hearts with dreams and yearnings for all the ways He can use us! (cf. Romans 8:28). And just because we *were* doing something and it was effective for God, doesn't mean we will *always* be doing that same thing, in that same way forever! Releasing these things continually to God helps us to carry them well and freely when the baton *is* in our hands. Instead of holding them tightly and confining the work of God through us to operate in one particular way. When we do this, it releases God to use us in all sorts of ways!

In our season living in New York, I was at a dinner party where I met a beautiful girl who was new to our church. She told me the story of how she and her husband had found our church and why they started to attend. She told me they lived on Long Island along with the rest of her family. And she told me about the church they had attended for years and how they had faithfully served. Then they heard about what was happening at our church and the way that God was moving. She told me she and her husband wanted to be a part of what God was doing in the city. She also told me that she used to be on the worship team at her former church and carried a great deal of responsibility there. Curious, I wanted to hear more.

In coming to our church, she felt God leading her to do it differently, to do something different than leading worship (even though she loved it!) as she had done at their previous church on Long Island. (This is very rare in the worship-leading world!) So, she joined the host team, which is responsible for welcoming every person who walks through the doors at the beginning and end of each service. She sensed that God wanted to use her to "touch every person." Those were her actual words. It moved me so much. She said that many of their friends and people who knew them while up on Long Island did not understand why she was greeting people and not leading worship. She said many people have asked, "Why aren't you using your gift?" or "I can't believe you left your position to be on a *host* team!" (As though greeting and welcoming people is an insignificant role. There is no insignificant role in the kingdom of God!)

Her response was so humble and beautiful, yet direct and confident, as she said to the people who questioned their sanity for moving, "You must think God can only use us in ONE way!" She said, with what I could really see was sincere with NO agenda attached to it, "We came because God said to come and to believe for Him to use our lives in a greater way!"

This is what it means to truly RELEASE to God all that concerns you. When we hold on tightly to what we have always known because it's "what we know" and we stop to ask God if maybe He could be doing a new thing in us and through us, we close off our spirit to the next prompting. God is always doing a new thing! But we have to learn to trust Him so that we can follow Him anywhere. We can move anywhere God says to move, work any job God says to work, give any amount of money God says to give, serve in any way God asks us to serve and be fulfilled in it! Why? Because we have let go. It is never about us, anyway.

"To release" means "to set free from confinement, restraint, or bondage"! I like that idea! I have found that as I mature, God asks me to RELEASE into His care the cares of my life, and it is becoming easier to do so. In 1 Peter, it says, "Humble yourselves, therefore, under God's mighty hand, that he may lift you up in due time. Cast all your anxiety on him because he cares for you" (1 Peter 5:6–7, NIV). I can't release *myself* from worry, but I can release my worries to Jesus and allow Him to set me free. I can't worry and trust God at the same time!

When we continue to be ruled by a lack of trust in God and fail to actively come against these things in our lives through Jesus, we are in bondage. It is possible to be a Christian and be going to heaven and, at the same time, be living a locked-up life. In Galatians 5, Paul warned the Christians of this very thing! He wrote, "It is for freedom that Christ has set us free. Stand firm, then, and do not let yourselves be burdened again by a yoke of slavery" (Galatians 5:1, NIV). Paul makes it clear that we have a choice: we can choose to be free, or we can choose to return to the old way of living before Jesus took control in us! It is a heavy burden to have to need all the answers before we can trust that God will take care of everything that concerns us. And yet, so many people do just that. They try to get their lives "right" before turning to Jesus. It causes us to walk around weighed down instead of experiencing the release of joy that accompanies real and genuine trust that He works while we walk! We can always choose to trust God even in the most difficult of times. Trust is one of the most crucial elements to going "into the deep" with God. There will never be a time when our trust won't be tested, but "thanks be unto God, which always causes us to triumph" (2 Corinthians 2:14, KJV).

LAUNCHING POINTS CHAPTER 3

- What areas of my life do I experience more fear and less faith? Take a moment right now to answer the question and then bring each place of fear to Jesus and ask for the victory over fear and worry and a fresh release of faith in your life.

- As far as my dreams and desires go, have there been places that I am holding too tightly to and trying to push through in my own strength? Write down the places that God shows you, be honest, and then release them to Him so that it will be His will that is done in your life and not your will that is done in your life!

CHAPTER 4

ATMOSPHERIC PRESSURE

As we continue to venture into deeper water, consider the ocean for a moment. Vast, deep, powerful, and alive, the ocean can be both stunningly beautiful and treacherous. And yet, so little is known about the ocean. It remains one of the last frontiers for Man to conquer. Many scientists and oceanographers say that we haven't even scratched the surface of all the mysteries of the deep! For years, it was assumed nothing could survive and thrive in the harsh environment of the deep ocean. The scientific community believed that, due to the lack of light and the crushing atmospheric pressures found there, it would be virtually impossible for anything to live. Many considered the environment to be far too extreme for life to exist.

Then scientists and marine biologists began to delve deeper into the oceans and seas. New technologies and scientific advancements allowed for deeper and deeper depths to be reached. The secrets of the deep ocean began to be revealed! Incredible discoveries were made, most notably, how unfounded and incorrect the initial understanding of the deep ocean really was. In fact, the further down we are able to explore, the more life we seem to find! However, it takes a different *type* of life to thrive at these levels. Only species that thrive *under pressure* can live at these depths. And this has been the problem for researchers and ocean-ographers—*pressure*. You see, it is pressure that has prevented researchers from being able to really study the deep parts of the ocean. Man simply cannot tolerate the crushing weight found in the deep ocean.

Essentially, according to the researchers at the University of Hawai'i at Mānoa, the amount of atmospheric pressure increases with every ten meters of depth reached. Go down twenty or thirty meters, and the "weight" you would experience is equal to having two or three "atmospheres" bearing down upon you (Exploring Our Fluid Earth, n.d.). It is hard for us to even imagine or relate to what that actually means. If you have ever swum to the bottom of the deep end of a swimming pool, you know what some of that atmospheric weight feels like. At one thousand meters, the atmospheric pressure is one hundred *times* the atmospheric pressure found at the surface. Now, plummet tens of thousands of meters, and you begin to understand the harshness of the environment that the deep ocean produces. It is truly an extreme environment.

I believe there is a parallel between this extreme environment and our relationship with Jesus. There is something profound here, a common thread we must understand as we head into the mea-sureless and deep places in God. *The deeper you go, the more pressure you will experience!* In the same way that the atmospheric pressure increases as you descend into the depths of the ocean, spiritual "pressure" will increase as you endeavor to go deeper in God. Sadly, this is where I have seen many Christians "get off the train." They abandon their journey with Jesus when they begin to experience "spiritual" pressure. Yet, this type of pressure is to be expected; the devil will never roll out the red carpet for you to step out into new levels in God! You WILL be opposed! There WILL be resistance! It's part of the journey when you really go after all of Jesus.

Spiritual Pressure

The apostle Paul experienced tremendous pressure. After his experience on the road to Damascus, Paul abandoned his persecution of Christians and the early church. As a result of his encounter with Jesus, Paul had a revelation: the very person he was trying to stamp out was the one person he needed most. Paul suddenly realized that the Messiah, whom he and the rest of Israel had been waiting for, had already come! When Paul encountered Jesus, he encountered the Messiah!

This revelation alone brought pressure. Before his experience on the road to Damascus, Paul (Saul at the time) brought pressure in the form of torture, death, and fear upon the early Christians. He was ruthless in his pursuit of those who had abandoned their Jewish faith in favor of this new and radical faith called Christianity. For Paul, this was complete blasphemy. This was outrageous! And he was going to do something about it. So, Paul pursued these "Christians," as they would later become known, with a tremendous drive to wipe them out!

And then he encountered Jesus! He had an undeniable and

supernatural visitation from Jesus Himself! And with Paul's conversion and transformation of what he now believed, the spiritual pressure mounted against him. The pressure he once brought to bear against those early Christians was now mounted against him. Paul described it as follows:

> Are they servants of Christ? (I am out of my mind to talk like this.) I am more. I have worked much harder, been in prison more frequently, been flogged more severely, and been exposed to death again and again. Five times I received from the Jews the forty lashes minus one. Three times I was beaten with rods, once I was pelted with stones, three times I was shipwrecked, I spent a night and a day in the open sea, I have been constantly on the move. I have been in danger from rivers, in danger from bandits, in danger from my fellow Jews, in danger from Gentiles ; in danger in the city, in danger in the country, in danger at sea; and in danger from false believers. I have labored and toiled and have often gone without sleep; I have known hunger and thirst and have often gone without food. I have been cold and naked. Besides everything else, I face daily the *pressure* of my concern for all the churches.

> **2 Corinthians 11:23–28 (NIV)**

This pressure drove Paul deeper to the cross of Jesus Christ. As we will see, spiritual pressure tends to do just that—drive us closer to Jesus!

A Purifying Work

Many of us love the idea of living a powerful and influential life for Jesus Christ. We want to live a life of significance so that at the end of our race, when we stand before Jesus, we can say that we gave Him our very best. I believe this is the initial intention of everyone who calls Jesus their Lord. Unfortunately, many well-intended people shrink back when they learn what the journey is going to look like. Especially when the word "cost" comes into play, when our choice of following Jesus begins to cost us something! (More on this in a minute!) When the pressure comes, and it will, our natural inclination is to do whatever we can to get out from under it and relieve that pressure!

Yet, I believe God wants us to be men and women who won't shrink back from this pressure. I believe there are many who *do* understand that something greater is happening here. And for those who are willing to endure the pressure, there are very real treasures and rewards. Isaiah 45 explains why, "I will give you the treasures of darkness, riches stored in secret places, so that you may know that I am the Lord, the God of Israel, who summons you by name" (Isaiah 45:3, NIV). So that we would know deeply that God *is* who He says He is. The pressures are real, to be sure. But so are the treasures that can never be found without going through dark times! Remember, Jesus said that in this life, we would have trouble. But then He said, "But take heart! I have overcome the world." John 16:33, NIV).

One of the ways the word "pressure" is described is as the

amount of force that is applied to a specific area. Pressure forces who you really are inside, your true life in God, to come to the surface. Add a little pressure, and you suddenly see what you are made of. The pressure squeezes that which has been locked up and entrenched inside of us to be released. The ugly stuff we manage to hold together and hide from view is dislodged because of the pressure. It really cannot happen any other way, unfortunately. It's called purification. If you heat gold or silver, eventually, the dross (imperfections) bubbles to the surface. It might have looked decent before the fire, but when it has gone through the fire, it is stunning. It is clear and shines beautifully! Heat is a form of pressure. And the pressure applied to the gold or silver through the heat burns off the impurities. What's left is pure gold or silver.

In the same way, Jesus brings impurities to the surface of our individual lives so that He can set us free to be more effective for His use. At the time when we are under pressure, it is not fun. It's not easy. But it is so necessary. And it seems like God never rushes. He takes His time. Why? Because He is thorough. He wants us free of impurities that will ultimately drown us if left undealt with. He lets the process run its course, and He uses the pressure to drive us closer to Him. So, while we are busy trying to get away from the discomfort of the situation, we need to realize that the pressure is God putting His finger on us. Not because He's mad at us! Often, it means we are heading in the right direction! The finger God is putting on us temporarily is for our GOOD! If we squirm and try to get out from under the pressure, we miss what He is actually doing: drawing us in. Pressure is a purifier. It causes what is underneath to come to the surface. In the Message Bible, James 1 describes it as follows:

> Consider it a sheer gift, friends, when tests and challenges come at you from all sides. You know that under pressure, your faith-life is forced into the open and shows its true colors. So don't try to get out of anything prematurely. Let it do its work so you become mature and well-developed, not deficient in any way.
>
> **James 1:2–4 (MSG)**

I like this version. It reminds us that we are under pressure but not to "get out of anything prematurely." In other words, let the pressure do its job! Stay the course! In the end, you will be mature and lack nothing.

Roots Are Revealing!

Pressure is what brings maturity and health into our lives! It is a vital ingredient to an effective and full life in Jesus Christ. Pressure is one of the greatest ways to check how healthy your own roots are in God. We all want roots that go down deep and hold tightly to Jesus. He is our stabilizing force. Our roots reveal our *real* relationship with Jesus Christ. What is *really* there; how we *really* are.

Shallow roots show and cause deficiencies in our lives. Roots have a direct connection to the life-giving source of God. In nature, they are the real indicator of how well a plant or tree is doing. When a plant has brown leaves and looks sickly, the problem lies down in the roots. I have lived in Virginia Beach for most of my life. It is located in a tidal basin along the southern coast of Virginia. In fact, the region is known as "Tidewater" and is comprised of the combined cities of Chesapeake, Norfolk, Portsmouth, and Virginia Beach. The nature of the area is such that there is water everywhere. Much of the vegetation is unique to the area because of the shallow water table. One tree in particular, the nesting pine, grows very tall and very quickly because the roots never have to go very deep or work very hard to hit water. The nesting pine is a beautiful tree, and it appears to be a solid tree. However, as soon as a storm comes through, these are the first trees to blow over! Their roots are weak and shallow. The storm reveals the nesting pine's true vulnerability. Drive around this area after a storm or nor'easter has blown through, and you will find nesting pines nesting across the roads and people's yards and houses. They make a huge mess.

This same thing happens with our spiritual roots. We can appear to have it all together. We can appear to be growing strong and tall like the nesting pine. However, appearances are actually a very poor indicator of our relationship with Jesus. Appearances are made up of what we *want* people to see in us. (Hello, filters!) We all seem to know how to "look" good when we need to. But the truth is, we are only kidding ourselves. One time of testing or spiritual storm and many of us fall over like the nesting pine. The Bible tells us what genuine fruit looks like as a result of our relationship with Jesus Christ (see Galatians 5:22–23)! Good fruit is the result of strong roots. Strong roots are the ones that have gone down deep into the earth. Spiritual fruit is the result of strong, healthy roots in Jesus.

But this takes time. Long before the fruit of our life in Jesus is evident, a deep, unseen work must take place. Our roots must go deep and take hold of solid ground. Even though no one can see our roots, our strength and health depend upon them. A healthy tree has healthy roots, and a healthy tree produces healthy fruit thanks to the healthy roots.

Let's consider the nesting pine again. I think it is interesting that one of the reasons the nesting pine's roots never go very deep or become very strong is because of the abundance of water. The roots never have to work very hard. They don't *have* to go down very far.

Those of us who have the privilege of living in the United States have so much available to us, spiritually speaking. There are churches everywhere! We can go to Bible studies and small home groups. We can access church services twenty-four hours a day on TV and stream everything possible from any device we have. There are preachers and teachers and 1-800 prayer lines. There are conferences and no shortage of speaker series to buy; we can even hire people to look up our scriptures, so we don't have to do the searching for ourselves! You can even hear a fiery message preached from a soap box while leaving a football stadium! (Can't promise that it's a good one!) We are literally inundated with opportunities to hear about Jesus.

Now, please don't misunderstand me. I *believe* in the local church and the powerful work being done by countless men and women who truly love Jesus and all the amazing resources we have to get the message to the world. I believe it *is* important to be a part of a thriving local church. This is vital to our growth in God. But like the nesting pine, we run the risk of having shallow and weak roots because of all the "water" around us, spiritually speaking. The key to real growth in God happens when the church service ends and we walk back into our own individual worlds—the neighborhoods where we live and the office buildings where we work. In our schools and places where we shop. And in our conversations with the people we know.

Real growth happens when we spend time with Jesus and then we reach out to others. Real growth happens when we raise our children and work on our marriages, especially during the difficult times. It happens when we wake up on the Monday morning *after* the big conference and seek to know Jesus on our own! We must remember that even though there is much available to us, none of it can take the place of paving our *own* path into the presence of God! No one can do this for you; no one can show up in your place and give an account for you to Jesus! Your relationship is between YOU and HIM, and what is either there is there, and what isn't there isn't there! It's up to you. And it is not easy. That's where the pressure is.

Conformity

Another area where we will experience spiritual pressure is in the area of conformity. The word "conformity" simply means "to be in agreement with or to become like someone or something." Whether we realize it or not, we are always in the process of conforming to or agreeing with someone or something! We do this for many different reasons, and not all of those reasons are wrong! For instance, we *conform* to a business dress code when we are at work. We *conform* to the fashion styles and trends, and the stylists tell us what is "in" for this season so we can look good and "stay relevant." We *conform* to proper etiquette when we go out to dinner at an upscale restaurant. (Hopefully!) And because we are always in the process of conforming in one way or another to something, I believe this one area is one of the most dangerous to us. Why? Because if we aren't committed to paying strict attention to what we are *allowing* to become part of who we are, it will become a very slippery slope. A slippery slope is never a good thing! It means we are gaining speed and going in the wrong direction. Let's look at what Paul has to say about this in Romans 12.

> Therefore, I urge you, brothers and sisters, in view of God's mercy, to offer your bodies as living sacrifice, holy and pleasing to God—this is your true and proper worship. Do not *conform* to the pattern of this world, but be transformed by the renewing of your mind. Then you will be able to test and approve what God's will is—his good, pleasing and perfect will.
>
> **Romans 12:1–2 (NIV)**

As Christians, we are to be a *living sacrifice*. What this big statement means is that we willingly hold nothing back and offer our WHOLE life to God. Maybe you can picture yourself being willing to *die* for Jesus, maybe someday in the distant future, but what about *today*? Are you willing to really *live* for him? To do things *HIS* way and make *Him* the center of every decision you make and every day you live? Believe it or not, this LIVING sacrifice part tends to be the hardest of the two options, *dying* for Him or *living* for Him. Let's talk about it. We *accept* the generous gift of salvation, and then we *respond* by willingly giving God access to every part of who we are.

It means we give Him the right to change whatever needs changing and transforming whatever needs transforming in us! It means that we lay down our way of doing things and our big opinions, politics (ouch!), and preferences, and we take up God's ways of living and thinking. It means that HE gets the HIGHEST place in our lives! It means we allow nothing to take His place, no voice or view to become louder than His. *This becomes an offering to Jesus.*

A sacrifice is costly. Jesus paid the highest price when He sacrificed Himself violently on the cross for our salvation. He CHOSE to willingly be beaten and abused physically, mentally, and emotionally! Then, He carried that choice all the way to die a very painful and SLOW death on the cross. There is no getting around it. It was and still is one of the most horrific ways to die. He sacrificed in a way that we will never be able to repay Him for! But what He does ask of us, in response to His sacrificial love, is the offering up of *our* lives willingly in surrender to *Him*. We are to "find out what pleases the Lord" (Ephesians 5:10, NIV) and then make it our life's work to put action to what we know is right with the *way* we choose to live and walk our lives out.

The pressure will come for all of us to remain true to what we have promised God as the days we are living in and this world's ways become darker and darker. This very thing is the sword that many who *say* they love Jesus will either die on (by walking away) or fight with (against every demonic agenda) in the days to come. Frankly, these days are already here! There are and *will* be decisions to make that *will* challenge what we truly believe and yield to. These are life and death decision days! Either we will water down what we believe to *fit the culture*, or we will stand and take our places *regardless of the culture*! Now is a good time to prepare your soul for the pressure that is already here and the pressure that is still to come. After all, as Paul points out, *this* is our spiritual and reasonable act of worship. The Bible is telling us that this isn't even an over-the-top ask! Paul calls it REASONABLE! (Appropriate or fair.)

How do we do that? How do we offer up our lives as a living sacrifice to God? The answer lies in conformity. I like the New International Version's translation here because it uses the word "pattern." We are not to conform to the "pattern" of this world. We are not to conform or bring our lives into agreement and cooperation with the world and this world's way of doing things. Which means, but is not limited to, the world's opinions, views, beliefs, mindsets, definitions, changes to the natural order of things and values, etc. Drilling down even further, it means we don't just take on whatever the most present and predominant thought the world presents us with as it attempts to serve up the "new normal" with its "new realities."

What is even more serious is the "different gospel" and the "different Jesus" that will be taught in the days to come. Let me explain because Paul gets specific and warns very clearly about this in 2 Corinthians, where it says clearly,

> For [you seem willing to allow it] if [a man, woman, or spirit] comes and preaches *another Jesus* whom we have not preached, or if you receive *a different spirit* from the one you received, or *a different gospel* from the one you accepted. You tolerate all this beautifully [welcoming the deception]. […] For such men are counterfeit apostles, deceitful workers, masquerading as apostles of Christ.
>
> **2 Corinthians 11:4, 13 (AMP)**

The only way to keep watch over our own souls will be to make a serious decision to continuously conform to God's way! Where we bring our lives UP to the standard of the Bible instead of attempting to bring the Bible DOWN to fit our standards! As we do this, we will learn how to measure every single thought and presumption offered to us by the Word of God only! If it doesn't fit, throw it out! The reason I believe conformity is so dangerous to the Christian life is because it is so easy to begin to try and mesh the pattern of the Word into the pattern of this world. (Never the two shall meet!)

We may feel confident that *surely* we would not miss it if someone was coming to us with a different gospel or spirit or Jesus, but conformity can be a subtle progression. The Bible warns us seriously in Matthew 24 that in the last days, even the elect (those who KNOW JESUS), if possible, will be deceived (Matthew 24:23). The good news is that it doesn't say that *every single Christian* will be deceived and miss the way. But it does tell us that *many* will be. It doesn't always start with the "big" things. We make little decisions and allowances along the way that seem "like no big deal." Maybe it starts with moving scriptures around to soothe our consciences when we feel convicted about something the Bible says! We start telling ourselves God probably didn't mean that. (To cast doubt on the legitimacy of the Word.) The devil will also deceive many by telling them things like, "God 'understands' that times have changed," "the Bible has evolved," etc. When we do this over time, we are actively plummeting into "another gospel" and "another Jesus." Each little decision, each little shift, has the capacity to deaden up our ability to discern truth from error! This is where the pressure is. Right here. Remember, it doesn't take much of a shift to end up in a completely different destination than the one you set out to reach.

You will experience tremendous pressure when you choose to go a different way than the one in which everyone around is going. Your friends want to go out and hang right on the line of morality (sometimes forgetting morality altogether and jumping right over that line and going right into the scene!), and knowing this lifestyle will ultimately take you down, you choose to go a different way. Maybe even losing friends as you do. Pressure. Your coworkers are lying and taking shortcuts that lower the ethics in their work, and you choose to do the right thing. You take the longer route but the honest route. Pressure. When all your friends (men and women alike) want to have a girl's night or a guy's night every week, and you are in an intense season of your marriage, so instead of escaping, you stay home or take your spouse out to prioritize your marriage. Pressure. The pressure comes as a result of your choosing to swim against the tide.

So, how do you avoid conformity to all the wrong things? You transform your mind. This is something that you daily *choose* to do! You renew the way you think by spending time in the WHOLE of God's Word. You renew the way you think when you refuse to cut and paste the Word of God! You renew the way *you* look at things by studying the way *God* looks at things. You begin to align yourself with what you *see* in the Word. Even when you are under pressure to conform to the patterns of this world, you will know how to *respond* to that pressure because of what the Word says.

I walked with someone who was close to me years ago as they went through a season of going their own way and went decidedly against all that they had ever believed and known was right. It was a devastating thing to watch. It felt like watching a train coming at full speed with someone standing on the tracks and not being able to do anything about it! I knew that, honestly, there was nothing that could be done but wait for this person to get to the bottom and the end of themself before they could really come to Jesus. Thankfully, after much prayer and a very real encounter with Jesus, I did get to see this very close friend come back to God. In those first few weeks and months after she decided to turn her life back over to Jesus, she experienced a real battle that was tormenting her deep inside. She had gone far down the road of regret, away from God over several years. And because of this, she had been conforming to the world's pattern for so long that it was a fight to rework the damage that was done in her mind and soul.

I remember one night we were talking about her mind, and in my attempt to encourage her, I was honest with her and told her that she would need to relearn to think God's way again. I told her that she really could do it! That God wanted to give her fresh eyes to see His Word with a new vision. That's when God gave me a picture of a wallpapered room. I told her what I saw. "Friend, it is a matter of the wallpaper in your mind right now. In a wallpapered room, all you can see is what has been glued to those walls for decoration, and it has become what you know and all that you see. But now, it's time to tear down the old wallpaper and put up the new!" I was thinking of the scripture in 2 Corinthians 5, where it says that if any man, woman, or child is *in* Christ, he is a *new* creation! The *old* has gone, and the *new* has come! (2 Corinthians 5:17). Later, I grabbed some other friends who went with me to where she was living, armed with scriptures, and we literally taped them to the walls of her room, bathroom, and kitchen! We "wallpapered" that home to help her renew her thinking. What about you as you are reading, do you need new wallpaper? Just like my friend, YOU can do it too! God can change and rework your mind!

As you renew your mind to the standards of God's Word, your desires and emotions will begin to change. They will transform. You will begin to think more and more like Jesus. This is what Paul means when he encourages us to be a living sacrifice. Pressure will always be the companion of sacrifice.

Enlarged Capacity!

We have discussed how pressure brings impurities to the surface for God to purify and how pressure causes our roots to go deeper in God! So, let's look at how pressure can enlarge our capacity. Advancements in oceanography and related technologies have made it possible in recent years for researchers to descend to previously unimaginable depths. We are now able to explore the many unchartered areas of the deep oceans. It is pretty amazing, really, to think of where we are now able to go.

However, to safely travel to these incredibly deep levels, the craft or vehicle must be properly pressurized as it descends and later ascends back to the surface. Improper pressurization or a rate of descent or ascent that is too rapid could be catastrophic. There is a process by which the vehicle and its occupants adapt to the new atmospheres at each new depth. Otherwise, they would literally be crushed. The gradual nature of the process of pressurization makes the new atmospheric weight and depth bearable. It can take many hours to descend to some depths. Pressurization is enlarging capacity.

Our journey into the deeper things of God is a *process*. It takes time. And because of the increased pressures we may experience along the way, we need to be properly pressurized. I am so glad God doesn't show me the whole journey all at once! Honestly, I probably wouldn't go if He did! God always works in us with the love of a Father, so He deeply cares about *how* we are doing along the way. This doesn't mean He will decrease the pressure, however. But He will strategically and consistently increase our strength to bear up under it! Paul spoke about this enlarging capacity when he wrote,

> But we have this treasure in jars of clay to show that this all-surpassing power is from God and not from us. We are hard pressed on every side, but not crushed; perplexed, but not in despair; persecuted, but not abandoned; struck down, but not destroyed. We always carry around in our body the death of Jesus, so that the life of Jesus may also be revealed in our body.

> **2 Corinthians 4:7–10 (NIV)**

Paul knew about pressure. He understood what it meant to journey to new places in God. He was stretched and afflicted. He endured all sorts of potentially crushing situations.

As Jesus walks us through times of great pressure into a deeper relationship with Him, He gives us His power and His strength to do what we cannot do on our own. When we are in a place that requires us to draw upon the strength of God to see us through, we enlarge our capacity to carry more weight in God! The more we draw upon God, the deeper He will take us.

Don't make the mistake here of thinking that by being enlarged and carrying weight in the kingdom, I am speaking about being weighed down. There is a difference! Being *weighed down* is something God never intended for us! Jesus tells us in Matthew 11, "I won't lay anything heavy or ill-fitting on you. Keep company with me and you'll learn to live *freely* and l*ightly*" (Matthew 11:30, MSG). If we are constantly weighed down, it means we are carrying the weight on our own and in our own strength, and we need to make the shift. We need to shift the weight back onto Jesus, whose shoulders were and will always be meant to bear our burdens. Humans aren't made to carry burdens. We are designed by God to release the weight onto Him. When we do this, we should feel a change in the pressure. The atmosphere will be different. Keep in mind that not every pressure you face is from God. (Refer back to chapter 2, "The Prompting.") The kind of weight that God enables His people to carry is the weight that brings growth and health to your life! He enlarges our capacity.

Getting into physical shape and exercising is something most people don't enjoy. Over the years, this has had to become a mind shift for me, and I enjoy it more now! I have to remind myself when I head out every morning to my gym that this is a GOOD thing! That in order to get the results I want, this is what it will take! I have to recommit to the goal. I've noticed that the more I go, the easier it gets to go. I've also noticed that each week, I can increase how much weight I can lift. What was once impossible to lift, in time, becomes possible to lift!

This is the kind of capacity God wants us to give us. When the pressure comes, we learn how to hold our ground, bear up underneath it and come through on the other side. We end up stronger! Paul wrote, "Therefore, my dear brothers and sisters, stand firm. Let nothing move you. Always give yourselves fully to the work of the Lord, because you know that your labor in the Lord is not in vain" (1 Corinthians 15:58, NIV). The pressure God takes us through always has a purpose. God always has a plan. It is never in vain! But we will need to train ourselves to stand firm. We cannot let anything move us. And as James encouraged us, do not try to get out from under it prematurely.

Atmospheric pressure is part of the environment in which God chooses to ready us! And just like the living creatures discovered in the deepest parts of the ocean, we too can thrive under pressure. Thankfully, God *does* give us places of rest, and relief *does* come. The pressure does not last forever! God would never leave us permanently in the press. If you find yourself in an intense season of pressure, take courage that Jesus is with you. Stand firm. It takes time to pressurize your soul, but it is so worth the effort and surrender. Know that you are going to new depths in God and that He will see you through!

LAUNCHING POINTS CHAPTER 4

- Right now, what areas are you experiencing pressure in the atmosphere of your life? Take a moment to think and then write them down.

- Do you know what kind of pressure it is?

- Who or what are you conforming to?

- After reading chapter 4 and considering the atmospheric pressure you have just identified, how do you feel God is asking you to respond right now to these pressures? Is there anything you sense God might be trying to say to you during this time in your life? Spend a few moments in prayer, write down what God is saying to you, and bring each area of pressure you are experiencing back into the care of Jesus.

CHAPTER 5

WHEN VISIBILITY IS LOW

As we continue into the deep, we need to look at the subject of visibility. Since being able to "see" clearly is a critical component of our spiritual walk, we need to know what we should be preparing for! Deep sea divers spend countless hours training in low visibility conditions. In fact, low visibility training is really what takes a potential deep-sea diver from novice to expert. How well the divers excel in learning to use other ways of "sight" when natural conditions deteriorate will determine how successful they will be in the deep!

Natalie L. Gibb, a certified Professional Association of Diving Instructors (PADI) member and scuba diving enthusiast, explains it as follows:

> Learning to use a variety of references to maintain orientation greatly increases a diver's sense of control and enjoyment in poor visibility. The most obvious references are a diver's gauges, including his depth gauge and his compass. A diver should be sure to check his gauges frequently during a dive in reduced visibility to maintain awareness of his depth and direction.
>
> **(Gibb 2019)**

Spiritually speaking, these simple diving guidelines are profound!

When visibility is low or poor in the deep, for a novice, it would be easy to become disoriented and make bad, split-second decisions out of panic, which would be the difference between life and death. The same is true about us in our spiritual walk with God. Stated another way, the devil hates the idea of sight! He's banking on us becoming disoriented with God, with what He is doing and what is happening in our lives! Using this sort of moment to throw us is just his style. To throw us in such a place that we make a bad, split-second decision out of panic that can have disastrous impacts on our life. But God has a way of escape for every trap the devil tries to lay for us! Let's take a closer look.

Blindness—Natural (or Physical) and Spiritual

All throughout the New Testament, Jesus healed people of blindness! And not just physical blindness. He healed people of spiritual blindness, as well. There is a great example of this in the ninth chapter of the book of John. Jesus and His disciples came upon a man who had been blind since birth. The disciples ask Jesus about the blind man, whether it was the blind man or his parents who had sinned and thus caused the blindness. "'Neither this man nor his parents sinned,' said Jesus, 'but this happened so that the works of God might be displayed in him'" (John 9:1–3, NIV). I love that last statement, "so that the works of God might be displayed in him." This is precisely why the devil hates the thought of us getting a genuine revelation of who Jesus is!

Low or poor visibility in our life can often come upon us suddenly and without warning. One moment the sun is shining, and everything is clear. You are feeling confident and secure in where God has you; your marriage is thriving, your work is rewarding, your relationships are healthy and fulfilling, and then—WHAT? The fog rolls in, and it doesn't seem to lift. There is a trial that never seems to end, a job layoff, a betrayal in a friendship, a change in income, or maybe the news of a devastating medical diagnosis. You can fill in the blank. Our sunny and clear skies suddenly darken.

It is in these very situations that we can become disoriented. Just as the weather can change suddenly and deteriorate, losing our sense of direction and purpose can overwhelm us in the midst of a sudden change in our lives! *Webster's Dictionary* defines "disorientation" as "mental confusion or impaired awareness, especially regarding place, time or personal identity." Disorientation can happen to the best of us.

I Can't See!

One particular Halloween a few years ago, my husband and I went to visit some friends in Montclair, New Jersey, for the evening. Montclair is a beautiful, storybook-type of town roughly thirty minutes from New York City. The houses are stunning, turn-of-the-century structures with wide front porches. The streets are lined with large, old trees and dotted with the most beautiful, glowing streetlamps. It is dreamy.

Anyway, our friends in Montclair had invited other friends we know from New York and surrounding neighborhoods to join us for dinner. Their house was a huge, possibly four-floor home. A massive turn-of-the-century house with all kinds of places to explore! We were enjoying the change of seasons as fall was rolling in, and it was one of the first cold nights. Everyone was having the best time as we ate and chatted and as we later sat with friends in front of a roaring fire in the huge stone fireplace. Most of the couples brought their children, and it seemed like there wasn't a corner of the house without a child in it! There were kids outside, kids on video games somewhere in the house, there was the room where all the babies were sleeping and some performance or "show" that was being organized in another area by and with most of the little girls! (We were all wondering what on earth that show was going to be! What we knew for sure was that WE would be their audience.) It was hilarious! As the evening lingered, it became dark outside. Really dark. And then it happened! The power went out! Suddenly, the children's laughter and their silliness turned into screaming and cries for help! Panic set in. The once happy and carefree children were now very much afraid. Because the house was so big and old, take the lights away, and it was SCARY for those kids! And their cries could be heard all over the house!

"Mommy! Mommy! Help me; I'm so scared!"

"It's so dark! Where are you? I can't see!" "Can anybody hear me?"

Parents scrambled! Thumping and bumping around (there is NEVER a flashlight when you need one!), every parent and adult went into total "calm everyone down" mode. We said things like,

"Everything is going to be fine!" "Even though it's dark, we are all still here," "I'm not afraid, so you don't have to be afraid!" And when all the children had been found and accounted for, you could hear them say, "I was worried I wouldn't be able to find you!" and "Can I sit on your lap?" The mood had completely changed. Not a single child left their parent's side the rest of that evening! It doesn't take much for us, as human beings, to become disorientated and confused. Throw in a little darkness, and we all become pushed to the brink. No one had to teach all those little children to be afraid of the dark! They just were. It was a natural reaction!

Navigating through periods of low visibility, or even total blackouts in our lives, we are forced to rely upon what we *know*. This is when to put into practice what we learned in the *light* so that we can navigate and find our way when we are in the dark! Low visibility is one of the obstacles every diver or ship captain must learn to overcome. They are trained in how to use specially designed marine instruments and gauges. Reliance upon these navigation instruments is critical! The natural inclination is to judge a situation based on physical sight instead of relying upon the readings of the marine instrument! And it takes special training not only to understand how to read the instruments and gauges but also to trust them!

In order to safely navigate into deeper waters, one would need a set of nautical charts, plotting tools, a compass, and perhaps even various types of electronic navigational equipment, including a radio and a depth finder! No experienced boater would head out into the deep without these types of tools unless they wanted to endanger themselves or the lives of the others with them on the journey. And the same would hold true for a deep-sea diver. Depth gauges and meters to indicate how much air remains in the air tanks are indispensable tools, to name just a few. It's one thing to have these types of tools and instruments on board; it is another thing to know how to put them to use and to put one's trust in them. And that takes training.

I believe there are ways to safeguard our lives when we come to know Jesus. And just like a ship's captain or deep-sea diver, there are certain things we need to learn in order to navigate through our natural world as spirit beings. We have talked about a few of these things already in the previous chapters. Things like hearing the voice of God and following His voice or learning to trust God and yielding to Him. We will discuss other areas in later chapters. The point is that, however, there are things we need to know how to do in order to navigate this life we are now living. This is especially true because the spiritual realm is the *unseen* realm. Our natural eyes can't help us. The Bible says that storms will come, that there will be times that the waters will rise, and the winds will blow. But Jesus always enables us and empowers us in times like these to use His ability, His strength, to use His eyes in order to find our way.

I want to stress again and again the importance of the "compass" of the Word of God in our lives! (The importance of the Word of God is a continuing theme in almost every chapter! Hopefully, you are understanding *why*.) Not only does the Word provide direction, but it also establishes boundary lines to prevent us from heading into dangerous waters. There have been times in my own life when I was not *seeing* in the natural what I knew to be true in the Word of God. Yet, what I knew and had hidden in my heart about God helped me to trust Him beyond what my physical eyes were seeing. I was able to attach my faith to His WORD, not my circumstance!

Even in the Valleys!

As I stated in chapter 1, I have amazing parents who love Jesus and have followed Him for years. My two sisters and my brother and me grew up watching them live out an authentic life in Jesus and what it means to serve Him. From a very early age, we learned from them who Jesus was and is and how to follow Him. They invested in us the things of God! And even though my parents were faithful to teach us about God, each of us still had our own choices to make and our own journeys in God to walk out. There were seasons when not everyone in the family was seeking God or serving Him! There were seasons when not everyone had the same revelation about Jesus at the same time. There have been mountain tops spiritually in each of our lives, and there have been some low valleys along the way. (Don't we all have mountains and valleys?) But I've learned not to be scared when a valley is up ahead because God has an individual plan and road for each one of us as our stories continue to unfold.

Years ago, one of my siblings went through what seemed to me to be a very long season of being away from God. They were young and doing their own thing. Honestly, at that time, they wanted to have nothing to do with the things of God. I was deeply concerned, and I worried about this much-loved member of the family all the time. I was newly married and living far away. It didn't matter how far away I was; I was worried and going down the whole "what if" road. I think I went down ALL the "what if" roads. I just couldn't understand how this could be happening, how they could just walk away from God. Why couldn't they see?

This period marked one of the first times in my walk with the Lord where I had to make a choice. Either I could remain confused—or disoriented—about what I was seeing, or I could open my Bible and read, again, the words of a promise that I love so much, "God is not human, that he should lie, not a human being, that he should change his mind. Does he speak and then not act? Does he promise and not fulfill?" (Numbers 23:19, NIV).

I remember one night praying for God to step in and turn this heart toward Jesus again. I opened my Bible to that very scripture and held it up above my head. I began to pray, "Lord Jesus, this is what your Word says! You have promised me that you don't change your mind! You don't change the plan just because it doesn't look right yet! And you have also said that when you make promises, you are prepared to KEEP them! I've seen you open eyes before; I pray that you would do it again now, in this present crisis! I won't give the devil this victory to take someone I love down a spiraling path! So, it is in these things that I choose to put my trust, no matter what I see. I choose to believe that you are over this circumstance and that every one of us will serve the Lord!"

I can tell you that God *did* hear my prayer, and my sibling *did* return to the Lord. Today, this loved one is serving God in all different arenas of life, and especially with their family, and in the power of God! I continue to be totally amazed by God's ability to weave beauty out of even the upheavals of life.

There was a breakthrough that God really gave me in that prayer and in my faith when I stopped relying on what I could "see" in the natural as it concerned my family and drifting away from God. I was encouraged in my heart that God had HEARD my voice while I waited for my miracle. God was teaching me how to *use* His Word to keep me from becoming disoriented.

The Word

Friends, yes, we are going back to the subject of the Word once more! Let's go further. We need the Word of God in the very same way we need air. This is the honest truth. We must *know* what it says, which means we will need to spend very real *time* reading and praying through the Bible. If you don't know what the Word says or if you spend very little *time* reading it and meditating on what it says, let me just encourage you today to make a "line-in-the-sand" moment in this area! Spend time in the Word! This is so important! I cannot stress this enough. There is no way to follow Jesus into the deep places in Him apart from His Word. As we have established, there are no shortcuts! In spending real and focused time with Him, you allow God to bring light and revelation into your world. I find it interesting that we make time to do what we really *want* to do, no matter what it is!

If you are hungry and desperate for food, you will find a way to get something to eat. If we *want* to do it, we find a *way* to do it! If you want time to have your hair done, get with friends, or go to the game with the guys, we make it happen. Yet, for me, when it comes to asking someone what their time with Jesus is like, there tends to be a lot of shrugging or saying they *don't know what to read in the Bible*, that *they don't do well in the morning*, or that *they are exhausted at night.*

Each of those things tells me one thing! We are great at making excuses and justifying ourselves to ease the conviction God is using to draw us back to Him with! The truth is, if we want to be real about it, many of us don't *want* to do what it will really take to truly know Jesus and live in the power and authority of God. It is a heart problem. It's a hunger problem. It's a lack of true desperation for Jesus. Why do we see God move miraculously in the developing world? I believe there is a level of hunger and desperation in those countries that we have yet to see here in the Western world.

For many in developing countries, life is touch and go at BEST. Many times, they have nothing. No place to live, nothing to eat. Literally nothing. So they come to Jesus with a different level of hunger. *They are all too aware of their need!* Both physical and spiritual. There are no fronts. There is no one trying to pretend they don't need anything. Some are often at the end of hope! And Jesus meets them right there. He responds to the *awareness* and *desperation* of their own need!

The church I love dearly, which we were a part of for some amazing years and I had the honor of serving in as the worship and executive pastor, is Crosswalk Church in Williamsburg, Virginia. I love the spirit and the heart of the lead and founding pastors, Mark and Pam Morrow, along with their whole family. They are like family to us! We remain close to this day. They have a genuine commitment to many of the nations of the world through missions, partnering alongside missionaries with boots on the ground. This passion in the pastors has spilled over into the spirit and the life of the church. Crosswalk Church was and still IS so determined to take its place to ensure the gospel is preached worldwide! Especially in places where the Word of God has never been preached before and to the many unreached people groups of the world. These tend to be some of the roughest places on the earth to get to, to be in, and to accomplish any specific work in!

One Sunday, it was announced that there was a real-time need in Northern India, specifically in the remote states of Jammu, Kashmir, and Himachal Pradesh. In these regions of India, there are still many people who have never heard the gospel of Jesus Christ. Our church had specifically adopted the Tarkhan people group located in these states. Crosswalk had been leading a project there for thirteen years already and had close relationships with the ministry leaders who live there! The Tarkhan people speak the Dogri language, and they had never had a Bible that was translated into their language before. Up until then, they had to read Bibles in

Hindi, which is not as familiar to them. Yet they STILL hungered while they struggled for the Word and did their best to understand what they could of a Bible not in their own language!

Our pastor put out a call to our church that Sunday that he sensed God was calling Crosswalk to pay for the translation, printing, and mass distribution of Bibles IN the Dogri language! This was an ambitious ask for the people of our church, and yet, there was so much excitement in the people to see this project through that MORE than enough money was raised, and the answer was on the way for the Tarkhan people. (I love an ALL-IN spirit in a church!) Our church was given an opportunity to be a part of the *answer* to the prayers of the believers there. The church was so willing to see this become a reality that MORE than enough money came in, and *fast*, for this project to be completed! Actually, too much money was raised; it was so far beyond what was needed that our pastor was *giving money BACK to the people* in our church! (Have you ever seen that happen? I know I haven't.) Honestly, in all my life in ministry, I had never seen everyday people with everyday salaries raise money so quickly and happily!

The Indian ministry leaders were so thankful that they asked Pastor Mark if he would come on behalf of our church to this very remote and hard-to-reach place to dedicate and pray over these Bibles at the outset of their distribution! They also were insistent on thanking our pastor in person. (Some of the most honoring and thankful people across the world are those who have almost nothing.) It was a rigorous trip that involved having to smuggle Pastor

Mark into the region secretly, and he could only stay a matter of hours because of how restricted and hostile it is to Christianity! There was worship and a great sense of anticipation in the people. As these beautiful souls received a Bible, Pastor Mark says that there was a silent hush that went over the group as they began reading their Bibles for the first time in their own language!

In that initial Sunday morning service, the atmosphere stirred something inside of me. There was an immediate revelation and awareness, in ME, that this was just a snapshot of the desperation of so many people around the world to know the Word. They are so desperate to hold it in their hands that they will even be willing to try to read and understand a Bible in a different language than their own. Sadly, while there are always exceptions to this, there tends to be a stark difference from what I see here in the Western Hemisphere!

When a short film was played for the congregation so we could get a glimpse of what this need looked like, it undid me. It was footage of a truck pulling into a village, much like the one where the Bibles would go to the Tarkhan people. It showed people unloading boxes and boxes of Bibles. As they handed them to the people, there was almost a frenzy in the atmosphere! These beautiful people rushed to the delivery truck, running after it, gathering others as they did. People were weeping, and when a Bible was given to them, they held it so close and stared in genuine awe at the cover. They stood and prayed out loud with everyone around, praying over each other (everyone at the same time), thanking and thanking and thanking God for answering their prayers, just to have a BIBLE of their very own! A dream come true! This is happening all over the world.

Many of us in those very first services were truly convicted of how much we take for granted what it means to *have* a Bible! After that short film was played for our church, even in the excitement of what we would get to be a part of, I sensed a pause in the room. It was a good pause. A needed pause. I would venture to say we were *collectively* convicted and maybe even embarrassed of ourselves. (No one said this, but it was a tangible sense in my heart.) In our part of the world, we have multiple Bibles in our homes and at our fingertips. We have different versions, different sizes and colors, and we never think about whether it will be in our own language! *No big deal*; it's just a given! In this faraway country, the most ordinary-looking Bible was the PEARL of great price. They would rub the Bible and hug it, so desperate for more of Jesus. My eyes feel hot with tears now, just thinking about it as I write this. I ask for forgiveness again for the ways I've taken the Word of God for granted.

What about *us*? Where is *our* hunger? Where is *our* need and desperation for the Word of God? These humble and beautiful people in Northern India, who will never be famous, wealthy, esteemed, honored, or told "how anointed" they are here on earth, have unlocked the secret to LIFE. It is in the Word of God. We have no real comprehension of the price that has been paid and is RIGHT NOW being paid by brave people all over the world just to get their hands on a Bible and distribute it to others. Even in the face of prison, brutality, and even death! And then I am struck by the lack of interest that I have seen with my own eyes, here in the Western world and even closer to home, within our own country, for the Bible. (*Owning a Bible and going to church does not mean there is desperate hunger within us!*)

In contrast, I confess that it scares me at times, as I work with people in my life coaching practice and through pastoring, how little of them KNOW what the Bible says! I'm scared for them. I see them as easy prey for the devil because they don't know how to fight. They don't know where the LIGHT to travel with comes from, and even if they do, apathy keeps it at a distance. Many have never *searched* the Word for an answer. I have had to unravel many compromised ways of living and believing with people who have bought into lies from the devil! They don't have enough TRUTH hidden inside of them to recognize the lies. And because the Word of God is "alive and active. Sharper than any double-edged sword" (Hebrews 4:12, NIV), it doesn't even matter what scripture you read; He will bring that Word to LIFE inside of you! God will light up His Word to you because He is always watching over His Word to perform it and bring it to pass in you! (Jeremiah 1:12).

Let it be said that the devil will always bring out his best attempts to distract you when you set your mind to go deeper into the Word of God. Be ready! *Expect* tiredness to rage in you, *expect* the phone to ring, and *expect* to suddenly remember all the things you need to do when you sit down to spend time with Jesus. I'm telling you these things are strategically designed by the devil to keep you AWAY from the very place where you will get breakthrough and become mature enough spiritually to learn how to silence him. Pray for your desire for God to be GREATER than any distraction strategies of the devil. If you aren't hungry, you can ask God to fill you with hunger for the Word. That is a request He can't wait to answer! As He does, be ready to *resist* the devil and every one of his attempts to stop your growth. Determine to press through and get to Jesus! He will show you who He is; He will open your eyes and cause his revelation light to illuminate every dark place inside of you. Countless times in my life, God has brought a scripture I have read to my remembrance at just the right time for my help, direction, and comfort! Psalm 119 says, "I have hidden your word in my heart that I might not sin against you" (Psalm 119:11, NIV). If there is nothing hidden in our hearts, there will sadly be no compass during the days when visibility is low. Again, Psalm 119 declares, "Your word is a lamp for my feet, a light on my path" (Psalm 119:105, NIV).

Friend, there is a move of God coming; it's in motion right now, even as you read this sentence! It will be unlike anything we have ever seen up until this very moment. I believe it will be unleashed as we "repent and do the things you did at first" (Revelation 2:5, NIV) when we return to the WONDER of Jesus. The WONDER of salvation and the WONDER of the Word.

Particles in the Water

Let's take this one step further. Let's look at something as seemingly insignificant as small particles in water. Suspended particles of sand, mud, clay, or other bottom sediments affect the visibility underwater in much the same way as fog affects visibility on land—distant shapes become colorless, poorly-defined shadows. Visibility reduction caused by suspended particles may be slight or severe depending upon the density, type, and amount of sediment suspended in the water. As an example, clay sediment will become suspended easily, will reduce the visibility to nearly zero feet in a few moments, and will remain in suspension for many hours. In contrast, sand does not become suspended as easily as clay, rarely reduces the visibility to zero, and will fall out of suspension in a matter of minutes (Gibb 2019).

This is a powerful thought, particles in the water. Small, seemingly insignificant particles suspended in water can actually become a danger for a diver! Why? It is a matter of perspective. The particles in the water change the diver's perspective. They alter greatly what the diver sees: shapes, colors, and distance. The diver's sight is suddenly hindered, even limited. It's amazing to think that a diver can become completely blinded and disoriented by something as small as particles suspended in the water.

As we go through life, we can all experience periods when the particles and sediments of life are stirred up, and we lose our bearings. If we are not careful, these seemingly *small* elements can become a serious problem for us in God. They can cause blindness and a change in the way that we see things, giving us a problem with our perspective. These particles and sediments can be in the form of disappointment, rejection, hurt, weariness, fear, anger, frustration and depression, low self-esteem, people pleasing, along with every other possible emotion that can "get stirred up" within us. The sediment then begins to line our spirits as we become wounded, disillusioned, angry, hopeless, offended, and even defeated. Just to name a few! Once the particles and sediments are stirred up and swirling around, we become subject to more build-up and less sight! We end up operating in the wrong way, looking at our world through broken, silt-laden lenses instead of healed and whole eyes.

Whether the situations of your life involve brokenness in your body or in your spirit, through our own choices or the choices of another, it is so important to truly allow Jesus to come in and bring real healing into your heart and into your memories. Don't just blow past what God wants to bring to the surface. If there is a place within you that is hard to unlock on your own, it is important to reach out to a pastor or leader, coach, or therapist if you struggle to navigate any traumatic memories. Invite a safe person to pray with you and over you as you walk toward healing. Many times God brings revelation about areas in our lives in which He deeply wants and needs to heal. Yet, we need to invite Him in to heal us, to enable us to venture further out in our journey in Him. Sometimes we don't even realize we have an area of brokenness that is affecting our sight! The revelation God brings about isn't to make us feel horrible and unworthy or to cause us to relive unnecessary pain, but it is always to bring healing. Remember, God always brings things to the surface so that He can heal us and remove the burden brokenness brings. Jesus said in Luke, "The Spirit of the Lord... has sent me to proclaim freedom for the prisoners and recovery of sight for the blind" (Luke 4:18, NIV).

Jesus wants to bring recovery and release to your life in the way that you see! God has given us Jesus to heal us everywhere we hurt. I would also encourage you again to speak with someone you trust about what God is showing you in different areas of your life in regard to emotional healing. Think about allowing and inviting someone to walk beside you and pray with you. Never be afraid to ask God if there are specific areas in your life that you may be unaware of that need His healing power! I have gone to the Lord many times in my life and asked Him to reveal to me those areas, those deep places in me, where I have been wounded or offended and need greater healing. He is so kind and gentle in the way He works. Sometimes He brings things to my mind that I have pushed down and even forgotten. He has brought things to my memory that affected me in some way, and I hadn't realized it. And with each area He has shown me, He has ministered His love and healing power. So, I encourage you to take the time, even this moment, to stop reading and ask Jesus to speak to you about your own life. He wants to bring you healing.

A whole perspective is truly everything when it comes to living long and well in Jesus. When we try to live the full life in God, as He intends, but look at our lives through the particles and sediments of life, our perspective can be affected and alter what we see of God. It is so important to learn how to recognize the times in our lives when the particles and the sediments are beginning to stir and we begin to lose perspective. These are the times when we need Jesus to help us see what He sees so that we can gain a right perspective again.

Victory and Vulnerability

I have noticed in my own life that after times of breakthrough and victory, I will experience a direct attack in the area of my perspective! This happens to many of us! You would think I would know by now to spot those times when I am most vulnerable, but it isn't always easy to do. The simple truth is that we are all subject to times when we get hit with a loss of perspective! For encouragement in times like this, I love to read and reflect upon the story of Elijah.

> Now Ahab told Jezebel everything Elijah had done and how he had killed all the prophets with the sword. So Jezebel sent a messenger to Elijah to say, "May the gods deal with me, be it ever so severely, if by this time tomorrow I do not make your life like that of one of them." Elijah was afraid and ran for his life. When he came to Beersheba in Judah, he left his servant there, while he himself went a day's journey into the wilderness. He came to a broom bush, sat down under it and prayed that he might die. "I have had enough, Lord," he said. "Take my life; I am no better than my ancestors." Then he lay down under the bush and fell asleep.
>
> **1 Kings 19:1–5 (NIV)**

Elijah was a mighty, mighty prophet of God! He experienced the power of God in incredible ways and brought this awesome power to bear against God's enemies. When he commanded the rains to stop, the rains stopped for three years! And yet, in this passage, Elijah, the mighty prophet of God, is running for his life! Ever felt that way? I know I have!

Elijah stops long enough to sit down under a tree and prays, "God, take my life!" What happened? What just happened to this mighty prophet that he would run for his life and then want to die? Elijah had lost his perspective! There is much more to this story, however. To understand the significance of what happened to Elijah, we need to look back at the events that led up to this stunning loss of perspective! In 1 Kings 17, Elijah declares to the wicked King Ahab that "there will be neither dew nor rain in the next few years except at my word" (1 Kings 17:1, NIV). And with the impending drought, God instructs Elijah to leave the area and hide in a ravine. So, Elijah does what God tells him, and he hides in the Kerith Ravine, where he has a small brook from which to drink. God then has ravens bring Elijah bread and meat each morning and each evening. Can you imagine that? Elijah has food brought to him each day! By ravens! Incredible!

Later, the brook dries up, and Elijah is instructed to go to a town called Zarephath, where God has commanded a widow to supply Elijah with food. While he is staying with the widow in Zarephath, the widow's young son becomes ill and dies. What does Elijah do? Elijah raises the boy from the dead! Again, this is incredible!

The Great Showdown

Then, in the third year of the drought and famine, God sends Elijah back to Samaria to King Ahab to inform him that God is about to send rain. Upon returning, Elijah learns that Ahab's wife, Jezebel, has been murdering the prophets of the Lord in the land in Elijah's absence. Clearly, she is not happy about the drought and resulting famine! Elijah has had enough. He meets with King Ahab and reminds the king that the drought and famine are not his fault but the result of Ahab and his family's rejection of the Lord. Elijah demands that Ahab gather the four hundred and fifty prophets of Baal and the four hundred prophets of Asherah and meet him on Mount Carmel. It's about to go down. And it's going to get ugly!

Ahab gathers all of the wicked prophets of Baal and Asherah and meets Elijah at the appointed place. Elijah asks the people to decide who they are going to follow: "If the Lord is God, follow him; but if Baal is God, follow him" (1 Kings 18:21, NIV). But the people said nothing. So, Elijah challenges the prophets of Baal and Asherah to a showdown.

> Get two bulls for us. Let Baal's prophets choose one for themselves, and let them cut it into pieces and put it on the wood but not set fire to it. I will prepare the other bull and put it on the wood but not set fire to it. Then you call on the name of your god, and I will call on the name of the Lord. The god who answers by fire—he is God."

> **1 Kings 18:23–24 (NIV)**

And so it began. The prophets of Baal and Asherah called upon the name of their gods "from morning till noon" (1 Kings 18:26, NIV). Not surprisingly, nothing happened. Elijah even makes fun of them and the gods, saying, "Shout louder! Maybe your god is asleep!" So, they shouted louder and danced around, cutting and slashing themselves in hopes of getting their god's attention. But nothing happened. No fire.

When it was Elijah's turn, he raised the stakes: Elijah built an altar to the Lord and dug a trench around it. He then had four large pots of water dumped on the altar and the sacrifice. He had them dump four more pots of water on the altar. He even had them do it a third time. Water ran down the altar, saturating the sacrifice and the wood and filling the trench. And then he prayed.

> Lord, the God of Abraham, Isaac and Israel, let it be known today that you are God in Israel and that I am your servant and have done all these things at your command. Answer me, Lord, answer me, so these people will know that you, Lord, are God, and that you are turning their hearts back again.
>
> **1 Kings 18:36–37 (NIV)**

And with a mighty rush, the fire of God fell upon the altar and burned up the sacrifice, the wood, the stones of the altar, the ground around the altar, and all of the water in the trench!

God won! Elijah then ordered the people to grab all of the false prophets of Baal and Asherah and to take them down to the Kishon Valley, where he summarily slaughtered the false prophets, all eight hundred and fifty of them. That's right. Elijah, under the power of God, single-handedly kills all the prophets of Baal and Asherah because of the wickedness they carried out in Israel and avenges the deaths of the prophets of the Lord. Then Elijah prays to the Lord, and He sends the rain! Once again, this is incredible! And it is an incredible victory for the Lord.

Cue vulnerability! But now Elijah begins to sink in his perspective. Queen Jezebel learns everything Elijah has just done and how he killed all the prophets with a sword. She is outraged! She sends a messenger to Elijah and warns him, "May the gods deal with me, be it ever so severely, if by this time tomorrow I do not make your life like that of one of them" (1 Kings 19:2, NIV). Now, in spite of all of the miraculous events God performed through him, Elijah is suddenly overwhelmed by the message from Jezebel. Jezebel's message becomes the particles in the water; the message stirs up the sediment. Elijah loses his perspective. The Bible says he became afraid.

He stopped looking at all that God had just done in demonstration of His power and began to look at the particles floating in the water. I can just imagine Elijah's thought process: "That wicked queen is going to kill me! I am as good as dead already. I'm in the desert; I'm sure I'll die. God just used me, but He's probably done with me now. What's the use? I just wish He would take me now!"

I love this story because it reminds me that even someone as incredible as the prophet Elijah can lose their perspective. It can happen to any of us. I am always amazed at how quickly I can go from power to self-pity in the span of about an hour! Elijah was not much different from you and me. Even after one incredible experience after another, and seemingly immune from the power of the enemy, Elijah receives one bad message from Queen Jezebel, and he is thrown into a tailspin. He lost his bearings. He lost his perspective and, consequently, acted irrationally. He took his eyes off his Source. He took his "eyes" off God.

The most effective way to keep particles and sediment from destroying your sight is to keep looking at Jesus. When I find myself slipping into darkness, when I feel like I am losing my perspective, I read Psalm 121. It is one of my favorites. "I lift up my eyes to the mountains—where does my help come from? My help comes from the Lord, the Maker of heaven and earth" (Psalm 121:1–2, NIV). David reminded his soul where His real help comes from! He did it over and over again. He lifted up his eyes. And trained his soul. This is so important. There are numerous places in the Bible where God challenges people to lift up their heads, to lift up their eyes, to look up! Why? You cannot see beyond your "right now" with your eyes looking down.

Looking down is equivalent to looking to yourself for your answer. When you look down, you see your own two feet. I don't know about you, but when I lose perspective and look down at my own two feet, I immediately feel like running away from the problem. That's what Elijah did! He looked down, saw his own two feet, and took off running. And he ran straight out into the desert, sat down under a tree, and asked God to take his life. That's what happens when you look down. You become the answer to your problem. On the other hand, God wants to be the answer to your problem. That is why He continuously says to look up, to lift up our heads. When we look up, we no longer see ourselves. Looking up is a way in which we can shift our focus, change our perspective. Look up and see yourself standing next to Jesus. When we are focused on Him, He gives us the ability to see things through His eyes. This is where the fog lifts, light comes in, and perspective returns again. Returning to the story of Elijah, 1 Kings 19 tells us that God didn't leave Elijah in that place of despair. God helped Elijah. He enabled Elijah to rest and to eat. He even sent an angel, who ministered to Elijah and helped him regain his perspective! Do you know that God offers the same help to you and to me? I'm so glad God never leaves me in that place where I feel lost, where I have lost my perspective! If we are having a problem with our perspective, Jesus stands waiting for us to come to Him so that He can give us fresh eyes again. To see our life, not through our broken eyes, but through His eyes of hope and love. The apostle Paul prayed,

> I ask—ask the God of our Master, Jesus Christ, the God of glory—to make you intelligent and discerning in knowing him personally, your eyes focused and clear, so that you can see exactly what it is he is calling you to do, grasp the immensity of this glorious way of life […] oh, the utter extravagance of his work in us who trust him—endless energy, boundless strength!

Ephesians 1:18–19 (MSG)

It's Not Just About You

It is so important to remember that our healing and restored lives, our sight and renewed perspective, aren't just for our benefit but for the healing of those people our lives will touch! Before we even touch this thought, I want to acknowledge anyone who might be in a place today where, if you could be honest, you don't *want* to care about the people down the road; you just want YOUR healing. (I get it. I've been there.) When we are right in the middle of a hard or even traumatizing experience, this is SO real and understandable. Jesus understands exactly where you are. If that's where you are today, don't lose hope. God can touch you wherever you are, with whatever you need on this journey. The truth is, it is wise to work through your wounds and allow space for God to bring more healing, before stepping out prematurely to help another before you are ready. No one is a finished work when we are used by God, to be sure. But we can be in a much healthier space to do it well when we give ourselves time to heal. Just know how deeply loved you and the heart of God is toward you no matter where you are in your journey! There is no rush to be at this step yet. Take all the time you need. There may come a day *when* God brings you through, and you may feel called to help someone else who is where you have been. Just know that nothing you are facing today will have been wasted. I love this scripture, "Lead out those who have eyes but are blind, who have ears but are deaf!" (Isaiah 43:8, NIV).

God wants to use your story and your scars to bring freedom and hope into the life of someone else coming behind you! (Some of those people might even be living in your house!) There is a critical responsibility before us to face the things in our life that are broken so that when we are healed, we can assist others. We cannot lead others out while we remain bound. If we are not careful, instead of wholeness, we will pass on our own problems with anger, our insecurities, our fears, and our doubts to others instead of our testimony of the power of God and how He brought us through. That is not going to be your story. If you let Him, God *will* heal you, and He *will* use you in the days to come! And when He does, there will be no question of who brought you out!

Jesus said in the book of John, "I am the light of the world. Whoever follows me will never walk in darkness, but will have the light of life" (John 8:12, NIV)! Jesus IS the light of the world. He made the way for us to get to Him, and then He uses us to BE "the light of the world" (see Matthew 5:14). He challenged His followers to LEAD. To take a world wandering in darkness and lead it to the light of His salvation. Our healing and our restored sight really aren't for us, in the end! (Sure, we can enjoy the benefits of living a whole and free life, but there can be so much more!) *Our* healing is really only half the story! Our visibility becomes clear when we look to Jesus and He heals our brokenness. We may be a little imperfect still, but when we focus on seeing others find a place of wholeness through Jesus Christ, it is worth it all!

> In my distress [when seemingly closed in] I called
> upon the Lord and cried to my God; He heard my
> voice out of His temple (heavenly dwelling place),
> and my cry came before Him, into His [very] ears.

[...] For you cause my lamp to be lighted and to shine; the Lord my God illumines my darkness. For by You I can run through a troop, and by my God I can leap over a wall. As for God, His way is perfect! The word of the Lord is tested and tried; He is a shield to all those who take refuge and put their trust in Him. For who is God except the Lord? Or who is the Rock save our God, The God who girds me with strength and makes my way perfect? He makes my feet like hinds' feet [able to stand firmly or make progress on the dangerous heights of testing and trouble]; He sets me securely upon my high places.

Psalm 18:6, 28–33 (AMP)

When God sets us securely upon our high places, as He did with David, then we can reach down and grab the hand of someone else and help them to reach a higher place. This is a part of going into the deep with God.

LAUNCHING POINTS CHAPTER 5

- Are there areas in my life where sediment and particles (i.e., bitterness, anger, resentment, unforgiveness, frustration, etc.) have settled on the inside of me? Take a moment to write down the areas of your life that God shows you and then invite His healing power to transform these places.

- Have I struggled with losing my perspective and becoming discouraged when I don't understand what God is doing? Write down your answer honestly, and then take the time to pray and ask God to give you a renewed sense of His presence and ability to truly work all things together for good in your life.

- How hungry am I for the Word of God? What changes need to be made in my life to make spending time with Jesus a priority? I would encourage you to find a trusted friend or mentor so that you can keep yourself accountable for this!

CHAPTER 6

OVERCAPACITY

Have you ever heard someone say, "I am in over my head!"? Or maybe, "I have reached my limit!"? If you are like me, not only have you heard someone say that before, but you may have felt that way, too, at some point in your life. Whether it is personal finances, starting over, trouble in your marriage or with one of your kids, or perhaps a situation at work, each of us has experienced something that has pushed us to the brink. We reach the end of ourselves.

King David certainly felt that way at various times in his life. Many of the psalms he wrote stemmed from the fact that he was overwhelmed by his situation. Read what he wrote in Psalm 61, "Hear my cry, O God; listen to my prayer. From the ends of the earth I call to you, I call as my heart grows faint; lead me to the rock that is higher than I. For you have been my refuge, a strong tower against the foe" (Psalm 61:1–3, NIV).

He obviously felt as though he was at the "end of the earth" and that God was far, far away. His heart grew faint. David had reached his limit.

I believe the real introduction to a deeper walk with Jesus happens when we find ourselves in those very places where it is too much for us. We reach a place of overcapacity. Like filling a one-gallon container with two gallons, it's impossible because the amount is overcapacity. Overcapacity in God simply means we have reached a place where it becomes clear that we have just moved beyond our comfort zone and stepped out of our depth. Overcapacity in God means we have reached the limits of our abilities and resources. We are all done. We've got nothing left. We've reached the end of ourselves, and we have no idea how to go forward. In fact, we may not even know what going forward even looks like, let alone how to do it! And then the thoughts start pouring in: "What in the world am I doing?" Or "How am I ever going to get out of this mess?" Or "Maybe it would be better to let someone who 'knows what they are doing' step in and take it from here."

Yet, everything I see about the real journey of life in the deep places with God is the opposite of this natural response. In fact, all throughout the Bible, God was consistently choosing to use people who were "inadequate" for the job. Welcome! We are all in this group. God kept picking people who were laughable at worst and unlikely at best to be anything God could use, yet they became chosen!

Consider Gideon. The angel of the Lord found him hiding in a wine press. Gideon was full of doubt and fear. And yet the Lord chose him to lead an army of misfits to fight the Midianite army. And then there is Moses, who complained to the Lord that he had a speech problem and was afraid of public speaking. God chose

Moses anyway, and he led the Hebrew people out of Egypt. Or consider the young woman, Esther. An orphan exiled in a foreign land, Esther was chosen to save her entire nation from genocide. Or Mary, the mother of Jesus. From a natural point of view, she was an unwed teen mother! Or consider the apostle Paul. Paul had a history of persecuting the early church and was known as an abuser and murderer! He was responsible for having many Christians put to death. And the list goes on and on of the people God chose for assignments of great significance! God seemingly picks ordinary people, who are arguably subpar, to do extraordinary things!

The real way that God works is to purposely take us past our abilities and into a place where we absolutely MUST rely on who He is! He takes us beyond our past and present failures and beyond our insecurities and leads us into the endless resource and power of HIS ability! He doesn't seem to notice how inadequate we are or how incapable we seem to be. He overlooks our faults and fears and chooses us anyway. Sadly, many of us disqualify ourselves when we look at who we are and how big the assignment is! We decide it's too big and convince ourselves that we have no right to think God could use us to change the world around us and beyond. Too often, we let the idea of being beyond our capacity or beyond our depth to be a good enough reason to sit on the shore rather than following Jesus into the deep!

Time to Go

One of the first times in my life that I remember God dealing with me in this area of overcapacity was in my junior year of high school. My family and I had just moved back to Virginia Beach, Virginia, from Chicago, Illinois, where we had lived for about eight years. Our time in Chicago was one of the most significant times in my life, especially in terms of my own personal experience with Jesus. My family and I attended a massive church in the Chicago area, and each of us was involved in one way or another. In the youth, God was moving in such a significant and powerful way. As I explained in an earlier chapter, the youth were exploding! We were so hungry for Jesus, and we knew He wanted to use US in a mighty way! Prayer meetings before church were quickly at TOP capacity, and as a result, we were experiencing the power of God in the most incredible ways.

People like me, young in high school, were being saved! Lives were being changed! It spilled over into our schools and neighborhood. Then one evening, when we were on our summer vacation in Florida, my dad announced we were moving! It was a crushing blow! I could not believe it! Moving? Seriously? But why? Why do we have to move now? In my young mind, I could not understand why God would want to take me out of such a wonderful place. I was angry and worried (of course) and couldn't see how God's hand could possibly be on this. After all, God had just begun to move in my life. He suddenly became real to me, and I wanted more of Him. "This isn't fair," I remembered thinking at the time. But regardless, we packed everything up and moved to Virginia Beach, Virginia!

I was crushed. I was so homesick for Chicago and for my friends and for the life I had left behind! Those first few months in Virginia were so devastating for me. I would come directly home from school and sob every single day. New city, new school, new friends. In many ways, it was more than I could bear. Yet, in the midst of all the feelings of sadness and grief, God began to speak to me. "Remember those amazing prayer meetings you would have before school in Chicago? Do you remember how the rooms you were given to meet in to pray before school could hardly contain all the people who wanted to come? I want to do that same work here, in Virginia Beach! Will you allow me to use you here, in this school now?"

I remember feeling overwhelmed. I still missed everything about Chicago and wanted what I had there. And now I had to start all over again. It just seemed like it was too much for me. Especially when it came to the process of starting over in my new school. When I asked one day about using one of the classrooms, I was told I would have to start a "club" and that in order to have a "club," I would need to have fifty other kids sign a petition saying they would want this type of "club." Immediately, I freaked out! "I don't know a single person, Lord! At lunch, I'm scared to go into the cafeteria! How will I ever get fifty whole people to sign a petition for something like this?" I was building a pretty good case to the Lord on how crazy an idea it was to start a "prayer club."

"Oh, and in case you have forgotten," I said to Him, "I am in high school, and this isn't even a cool club!" But Jesus was with me. On I went into that cafeteria full of people that I didn't even know and got fifty signatures! I then had to go alone to the student council to present my "reasons" for this "Before School Prayer Club;" my voice shook as I had to speak. But because God's plans always prevail, I was approved to launch a prayer club in my high school!

Sometimes, we so easily forget that God never *really* needs our ability when He is asking us to do something! He is looking for someone to say, "YES! You can use me!" God is asking for our willingness to do what He asks, regardless of whether we think we have anything going for us or not! In fact, I think He actually likes it better when we have less to bring to the table! Why? Because it means we will have to be more dependent upon Him! It gives Him room to bring HIS ability and power to the situation. He adds what He can do to our willingness, and in that moment, something supernatural is released! "God is able to make all grace abound toward you, so that you in *all things* at *all times*, having all that you need, you will abound in every good work!" (2 Corinthians 9:8, NIV).

God moved me out of what seemed like the best environment to be in when He took me away from my life in Chicago and moved me to Virginia Beach. But what He was really doing was taking me into a new place of boldness in Him. He was walking me into my first defining moment! In Chicago, I was okay in the water up to my ankles. In Virginia Beach, God moved me out into deeper water; He moved me into water that was up to my knees. He took me from where I was familiar and comfortable to a place where I was unfamiliar—and definitely uncomfortable. He led me into deeper water. But Jesus brought me everything I needed to back up and support everything He was asking me to do!

In chapter 2, "The Prompting," I spoke about a time early in my life when I was learning to hear from God, and I would wake up in the night. God was teaching me how to hear! Then, as I became sensitive to the Holy Spirit, I learned to hear in many other ways. In the same way, I have learned how to respond to the times in my life when I have exceeded my capacity and faced overcapacity. My experience in high school to start a new prayer club in a new school in a new city was just the first of many experiences where God has asked me to allow HIS strength to take me beyond my natural ability! Instead of disqualifying myself from taking part in the great plan of God and convincing myself that what it is He is asking of me is something I am unable to do, God has taught me how to stop and remind myself of His promises. Consider what Paul wrote in II Corinthians: "But he said to me, 'My grace is sufficient for you, for my power is made perfect in weakness.' Therefore I will boast all the more gladly about my weaknesses, so that Christ's power may rest on me" (2 Corinthians 12:9–11, NIV). Like Paul, I am learning to boast about my weaknesses.

Self-Sufficiency versus Total Dependency

Self-sufficiency can be a serious problem when it comes to our relationship with God; He wants us to be dependent upon Him.

It slows things down when we are in a constant power struggle with God! He will always put His finger on our self-sufficiency when it comes up in our lives. *Webster's Dictionary* defines "self-sufficiency" as "being able to maintain oneself or itself without outside aid: capable of providing for one's own needs: having an extreme confidence in one's own ability or worth." Self-sufficiency is a dangerous problem because it reveals the problem of pride. Self-sufficiency becomes prideful when we rely on our own strength or take matters into our own hands. It's an "I've got this, God!" attitude. And this kind of attitude means trouble because it can open a door to the enemy. (It's the "door" conversation again!) The devil is always seeking to shroud and distort the actual truth in our lives. When we experience a victory in a particular situation, the devil will attempt to turn that victory into a "pride show" because that is actually *his* nature and *his* history! He will try to get us to take credit for what we just experienced. As we become aware of those times when self-sufficiency is beginning to take root in our lives, we must move quickly to uproot it. This form of pride will always cause a blockage and limit God's ability to use our lives for His purposes. We have to deal with self-sufficiency and the pride it can generate.

When God moves us into seasons of blessing or when God uses us in some way, it can be easy to look back and want to take some of the credit! To believe "all the news" about ourselves. We want to drink down every bit of praise given to us about us! But it's a *toxic cocktail* should we truly drink it down. We will need to resist this demon-inspired tendency of ours to take the glory. It is

God's power that causes something to come to life or a situation to turn around. We can never forget that apart from Him, we can do nothing! (cf. John 15:5). It's time to get wise about how pride offends God and how quickly the devil works through a puffed-up spirit.

The fourth chapter of the book of Daniel relates one of the most sobering accounts of how seriously God takes the sin of pride in our lives. Nebuchadnezzar was an evil king who often had dreams and visions that he was unable to interpret or understand. Daniel, a prophet of God and an exile in a foreign land, happened to be the only one in the entire country who could provide the interpretation and meaning. This way, Nebuchadnezzar would know that it was the Lord God who was speaking to him. On this particular night, King Nebuchadnezzar has a disturbing dream. He is truly frightened. He summons all of the wise men of Babylon to come to the palace in order that they might interpret the dream. But they are unable to understand the dream or provide its meaning. Daniel is then summoned to the palace. Again, this is a sobering tale, and it is worth reading the entire story of Nebuchadnezzar's dream. Let's pick it up in verse 19.

> Then Daniel (also called Belteshazzar) was greatly perplexed for a time, and his thoughts terrified him. So the king said, "Belteshazzar, do not let the dream or its meaning alarm you."
>
> Belteshazzar answered, "My lord, if only the dream applied to your enemies and its meaning to your adversaries! The tree you saw, which grew large and strong, with its top touching the sky, vis-

ible to the whole earth, with beautiful leaves and abundant fruit, providing food for all, giving shelter to the wild animals, and having nesting places in its branches for the birds—Your Majesty, you are that tree! You have become great and strong; your greatness has grown until it reaches the sky, and your dominion extends to the distant parts of the earth. [...]

This is the interpretation, Your Majesty, and this is the decree the Most High has issued against my lord the king; you will be driven away from people and will live with the wild animals; you will eat grass like the ox and be drenched with the dew of heaven. Seven times will pass by for you until you acknowledge that the Most High is sovereign over all kingdoms on earth and gives them to anyone he wishes."

Daniel 4:19–22, 24–25 (NIV)

The prophecy concerning King Nebuchadnezzar happened just as God had said, and for seven years, Nebuchadnezzar lived like a wild animal as Daniel had prophesied until God restored Nebuchadnezzar's sanity! The following is what Nebuchadnezzar later described:

At the same time that my sanity was restored, my honor and splendor were returned to me for the glory of my kingdom. My advisers and nobles sought me out, and I was restored to my throne and became even greater than before. Now I, Nebuchadnezzar, praise and exalt and glorify the King of heaven, because everything he does is right and all his ways are just. And those who walk in pride he is able to humble.

Daniel 4:36–37 (NIV)

What had happened with King Nebuchadnezzar was that he began to "read his own press," so to speak, and elevated himself to a place of such status that he was overtaken with pride. God was so sickened by this that He was compelled to take Nebuchadnezzar down an extremely humbling road for seven years before that spirit was broken in him. Pride is something that can creep into just about every area of our hearts and take over. Sometimes we don't even realize that pride has moved into our hearts! But there are some telltale signs. Elements of our personality can begin to display characteristics of pride:

A quick temper: "Where is your common sense? Anyone with half a brain could get this done! Get moving!"

Impatient: "If I were running this place, it would work like a well-oiled machine! This is ridiculously slow and a waste of my time!"

Elitism: "I've worked hard to be where I am; I should be honored!"

Preferred honor: Giving honor to those you think deserve it while ignoring and mistreating others.

Demanding: Pushy in your dealings with people and being a bully.

Argumentative: "I have to be right!" (Even if it crushes or destroys the other person.)

Self-seeking: "How can I be elevated and better seen by others?" (Hello, social media!)

Pushing your way to the front: Overly concerned about status and appearances.

Unmerciful: Withholding grace for someone else's failure or mistake or shortcoming.

I imagine there are many more signs and manifestations of pride, but these certainly top the list. How about you? Can you identify anything of yourself with any of these signs? In Philippians 2, in The Message Bible, Paul talks about the nature of Jesus.

> If you've gotten anything at all out of following Christ, if his love has made any difference in your life, if being in a community of the Spirit means anything to you, if you have a heart, if you care—then do me a favor: Agree with each other, love each other, be deep-spirited friends. Don't push your way to the front; don't sweet-talk your way to the top. Put yourself aside, and help others get ahead. Don't be obsessed with getting your own advantage. Forget yourselves long enough to lend a helping hand.
>
> Think of yourselves the way Christ Jesus thought of himself. He had equal status with God but didn't think so much of himself that he had to cling to the advantages of that status no matter what. Not at all. When the time came, he set aside the privileges of

deity and took on the status of a slave, became human! […]

Because of that obedience, God lifted him high and honored him far beyond anyone or anything, ever, so that all created beings in heaven and on earth—even those long ago dead and buried—will bow in worship before this Jesus Christ, and call out in praise that he is the Master of all, to the glorious honor of God the Father.

Philippians 2:1–11 (MSG)

Friends, our lives are most useful to Jesus when they line up with what Paul describes here in this passage of Philippians. Imitating the life of Jesus with the spirit in which He lived it out is the assignment of every believer!

This is exactly why God loves places of overcapacity. Overcapacity reminds us of who we are and who God is. It challenges the order in which we have been placing our own importance and puts Jesus in His rightful place of honor in our lives—on the throne! I can tell you that there have been countless times in my own life since that first "in over my head" experience in high school that God has asked me to come out and be used in a place I could have never succeeded in my own strength. Every time I reach that "in over my head" place, I have to face the giant of intimidation and press into Jesus. I can honestly say that in every story in my life where I yielded, Jesus has more than enabled me to do whatever He has asked me to do! And I believe He will do the same in you! Because when we have reached our overcapacity, He gets every ounce of the glory!

LAUNCHING POINTS CHAPTER 6

- Can you think of a situation right now in your life where you feel you are at "overcapacity"? How have you been dealing with it? Give an honest report of yourself and begin to ask God where you need to make a change.

- Write down some of the areas in your life where you feel you may be operating in self-sufficiency instead of total dependency on God.

- Write down what God shows you. Then take some time to pray and ask Him to help you learn how to draw on His ability to do for you in your life what you cannot do for yourself in your own strength.

CHAPTER 7

OFF THE MAP

Off the map. Have you ever gone off the map? Ever found yourself lost, and while looking at the map, you realize you're not even on the map? That's what it means to be "off the map." It's a place most of us try to avoid, and out on the deep ocean, you definitely don't want to be there without some chart or map. To be sure, no one likes the idea that they are suddenly lost. It is a horrible—even terrifying—feeling. "Off the map" takes us into the unknown, into the uncharted, to places where there is no guarantee of our safety or success! Yet, this is the very place God takes us when He wants us to go further into the deep. It's in the uncharted areas of our lives where God shows us who He is. It is where we use what we know in combination with the supernatural power of God to find our way into the land that we have been promised! Stated another way, "off the map" is where His "super" falls on our "natural" and the "supernatural" happens.

In 2011 as I've previously said, my husband, Paul, and I moved to the New York City area, and from the word go, it is marked as one of our greatest adventures so far! It did not take very long, however, before we realized how desperately we needed a trustworthy navigational device! Keep in mind that the iPhone wasn't what it is now! This was over twelve years ago. People were still buying separate navigational systems. The problem was, we waited for a little too long before we got it. (Realizing there is a problem and doing something about it are often two different things!)

Anyway, not long after we had moved to New York City, I drove out to New Jersey to visit a new friend. Later that night, as I was driving back home, I suddenly became very confused about where I was and ended up completely lost. I had gone "off the map" completely, and I panicked! It was dark, and I was alone. And to make matters worse, I couldn't find any gas stations that were open or any stores. I was totally lost! Oh, and the GPS device Paul and I constantly talked about getting for the car? Well, we never got it. So, there I was, lost in New Jersey. It was late and very dark, the gas stations were closed, and Paul still needed to buy me my navigational device. As I previously mentioned in one of the other chapters of this book, I like a good plan. I don't like surprises. I like organization. I like it when directions are clear and I can follow them.

When the plan and the map become irrelevant, we are forced (like I was on that New Jersey highway) to use a different set of tools to find our way! Thankfully, "the set of tools" I chose that night involved looking for the skyline of New York City in the distance and driving toward it! (Pitiful, I know!) Scarred, I did find my way home that night and vowed to never try that again without the best navigation system I could find!

Nothing in our human nature likes being dropped into the unknown. If we are given a choice between a clearly defined path and an unmarked map, most of us will pick the clearly defined path because it represents something we can wrap our heads around. So why is a journey "off the map" so important to God? Why does it seem that so many of the great men and women who have gone before us in God tell of braving unmarked territory? The answer is pretty simple. There are places in our souls that can only be worked out when we are taken to a destination off the map. This is the place where our comfort is challenged, where our needs are met by God alone, and where supernatural doors are opened before us!

The Uncomfortable Places

This is exactly the place God took the children of Israel when He was leading them out of the slavery and oppression of Egypt and into the land He had promised them all along. God had His reasons for taking them off the map. "When Pharaoh let the people go, God did not lead them on the road through the Philistine country, though that was shorter. For God said, 'If they face war, they might change their minds and return to Egypt.' So God led the people around by the desert road toward the Red Sea" (Exodus 13:17–18, NIV). There is one thing in which we can always be certain: whatever God does, it is always for our good. He knew what state the children of Israel were in, and He knew that the shorter route would ultimately cause their devastation. He knew that their faith was weak and that the temptation to return to what they had "known" in Egypt would be too much for them even though Egypt had been a place of captivity and bondage for them.

(Isn't it so like the devil to tell them to go back?) God will never tell us to go *back* into captivity; He only takes us into places of more and more freedom.

God knew the children of Israel would quickly crave the life of bondage they had just left the moment their comfort was challenged. Captivity and bondage in Egypt were all they had known for the previous four hundred and thirty years. Compared to the uncharted wilderness that lay before them, God knew the people of Israel would immediately fall back to what they had known, as uncomfortable as it was, rather than venturing forward into the unknown. These things would have to be addressed before they could enter into the life that God had planned for them.

So much of our life is built around our being comfortable! We spend more money than we are even close to being aware of on our own personal comfort! Products will sell, and we will buy them if they can increase comfort, speed up the comfort process, or make our comfort last longer! *Webster's Dictionary* describes "comfort" as "being in a state of ease and freedom from pain or constraint." It is a place of ease, convenience, and relief. Uncomfortable or discomfort, then, are simply the opposite of comfort. A discomfort is a place of pain, constraint, inconvenience. While comfort is being in a state of ease, there is nothing easy about the state of discomfort. Often uncomfortable descends into unbearable.

Off the Map and Uncomfortable

Those of us living in the United States or much of the Western world, for that matter, have never truly experienced the levels of discomfort that so many people around the world experience daily. Sure, we have rough areas in our cities and towns throughout the country, areas gripped by poverty and crime, where hopelessness abounds. Yet, even these places pale in comparison to many parts of the developing world, as we talked about in an earlier chapter. It's easy to think how hard we have it when faced with some inconvenience or momentary hardship. The truth is most of us have never really been exposed to the hardships others must endure.

Not long ago, I had the privilege of spending time and doing some ministry work with a wonderful organization in Denpasar, Indonesia, a foundation that rescues and cares for orphans in Indonesia. An Indonesian pastor and his wife, who I had the privilege of serving alongside while I was there, started the foundation when they were led off the map and into the deep! Caring for orphans became their life's calling. This couple already had two amazing daughters and asked now that God would bless them with a son! The pastor said, "I would see my neighbor playing outside with his little boy, and I wanted a boy as well!" Some time later, his wife became pregnant, and they were convinced that this was God's answer to their prayer for a son.

During the pregnancy, they went on a very long ministry trip as part of their work. They were gone, perhaps, too long. When they returned to their home, the pastor's wife experienced a miscarriage and lost their baby. Their dreams of a son were shattered. They were devastated. Yet, they continued to trust God. They thought that, perhaps, they should be content with the two children God had already given them. After all, their two beautiful daughters brought them so much happiness. They felt very blessed.

Months later, at the time when their baby would have been born, the pastor's wife received a phone call from a woman who learned that she and her husband were pastors of a church. The woman asked her over the phone, "Do you want a baby boy?" Obviously, she was shocked! She put down the phone and ran to call her husband! After an excited and joyous exchange, the pastor said to his wife, "Yes, let's take him home!" Three weeks later, another call came from a different mother who explained she could no longer care for her child. "Do you want another baby?" the mother asked in earnest. "I have a baby boy."

The following week, the couple received yet another phone call. "Do you still have room for another baby boy?" The pastor said that in that first year, they rescued sixteen babies! He said, "God, this isn't what I meant! I just wanted ONE baby boy!" Did they want a baby boy? God brought them baby BOYS! It started when this couple chose to trust God. The pastor laughed as he described how noisy their home became! He said he realized that God was speaking to him and that he knew God was doing something major. He admitted he didn't realize how major. God was calling them to rescue orphans. They had to start a foundation because their personal home was not large enough to accommodate all the children who would need to be rescued! The couple discussed how much work he knew it would be to undertake what

God was asking them to do. He was honest when He explained to God that he didn't really want to do it! He said, "I didn't want to do it because I didn't want to get that busy!"

But God continued to show this willing couple children who were in desperate need of rescue and that He had a major part for them to play in this great work. The pastor remembers the day when he finally surrendered to what God was asking them to do. "Okay, God, but I don't know how to start a foundation. I don't know how to do what this will take, but I know You will help me, so I will do it." From that moment, these pastors surrendered their comfort, and their rescue foundation was born. Today, there are well over twelve orphan homes across Indonesia because they said, "Yes!" They are building children's centers and shelters for women all over the country as they expand to meet their needs!

As I listened to the pastor share his story with me and experienced the work he and his wife were doing as they lived out the message of the kingdom of God, I sensed God place a challenge in my soul to war against my own desire to be comfortable. When God expands our hearts and our calling, He will always challenge our comfort. Growth happens when we become uncomfortable! This is what causes us to step out into new territory. God uses this great discomfort to determine how willing we are to follow Him. He uses it to strengthen our SOUL in weak areas. He uses it to show us what is really in our hearts. Sometimes He is forced to make it really uncomfortable. "Remember how the Lord your God led you all the way in the wilderness these forty years, to humble and test you in order to know what was in your heart, whether or not you would keep his commands" (Deuteronomy 8:2, NIV).

It is natural for us to want to pick the easy route, like pulling up to the drive-through window at a fast-food restaurant. We would naturally choose the plan with the least physical strain and pain from the menu board. "Oh, and I have a coupon, so I don't have to pay the full price, right?" The problem is this plan, this "happy meal," cannot be found in the Bible! There is no *cheap* version of a poured-out life. Instead, the Bible promises in Matthew 7:13–14 (NIV), "Enter through the narrow gate. For wide is the gate and broad is the road that leads to destruction, and many enter through it. But small is the gate and narrow the road that leads to life, and only a few find it." There are no coupons or value meals when it comes to following Jesus. The *value* comes from the *full price*.

The Narrow Road

In fact, the road is narrow because it involves sacrifice. It is where we lay down our rights and preferences, where we are told to deny ourselves and take up our cross and follow Jesus (see Matthew 16:24). The way of the cross will always require sacrifice. And because the way of the cross involves sacrifice, few find it! It's a lonely road at times. It isn't crowded when you travel this way. Look at the story of Jesus. When Jesus laid down His life, very few people were there with Him during His darkest moments. Sacrifice makes the human soul uncomfortable. We resist getting our hands dirty in the work of God. It isn't pretty, it definitely isn't convenient, and it will always cost us something. The Bible says that in the garden of Gethsemane, Jesus, knowing what He was about to face, prayed, "Not my will, but yours be done" (Luke 22:42, NIV). Sacrifice over comfort. This is the real way of the kingdom of God.

If you take a look at the first-century church and the first "Christians," a person would have had to count the cost in a very real way from the moment of their conversion. There was no visit from the local pastor or small group leader; there was no presentation of a Bible or Bible study program with help for your "next steps" with Jesus, or worship music, a streaming link with quick access to the pastor's latest inspiring message as we see in today's current church. In fact, there was nothing external that would have drawn anyone to be an early Christian! There were no perceived benefits, naturally speaking. Instead, the early Christians likely were captured by a group of soldiers and escorted to an arena where they faced torture, or imprisonment, beatings and burnings, and martyrdom, among other things. Persecution was a reality and a serious aspect of any person's decision to confess Jesus as Lord and Savior and then to follow Him, especially during the first century.

These early Christian believers faced incredible difficulties. Only a very real personal encounter and revelation of the living Jesus could have drawn someone to follow Him! Encouraged by letters from Peter, James, John, and others, they did not shrink back in their faith. The apostle Paul wrote two letters from his prison cell in Rome to his friend and protégé, Timothy, encouraging him and other believers to "Join with [him] in suffering, as a good soldier of Christ Jesus" (2 Timothy 2:3, NIV)! The writer of the book of Hebrews described in graphic detail the prospects of early Christian followers,

> Some faced jeers and flogging, and even chains and imprisonment. They were put to death by stoning; they were sawed in two; they were killed by the sword. They went about in sheepskins and goatskins, destitute, persecuted and mistreated—the world was not worthy of them.

Hebrews 11:36–38 (NIV)

Today, over 360 million Christians worldwide suffer some form of persecution because of their faith, according to statistics from the last decade (Persecution.org 2006). And this number is rising every day. As we speak, people all over the world are choosing to follow Jesus under the worst possible circumstances, enduring the immediate suffering for the JOY of eternity that is set before them.

Friends, while we are busy worrying about where our seat is in church on Sunday, or whether we liked the pastor's message or not, whether we "gained" anything from it or not, or if we liked the music during worship, other believers around the world suffer persecution and even death as they give up their lives in martyrdom for the sake of the gospel and their faith in the name of Jesus!

I am always challenged and convicted when I sit with people like these Indonesian pastors or when I read about the martyrs of the early church and the way in which they poured out every ounce of their blood to spread the good news of salvation through

Jesus Christ. Revelation 12:11 speaks of the sacrifices yet to come for the believers who will defeat the devil in the final battle. It tells us that they did not love their lives so much that they were afraid to die. Every time I read this, I ask God for strength and courage to make me willing.

Whether God asks us to give up our very lives or whether to simply sacrifice our time or substance for the sake of some soul in need of salvation, our prayer must be, "Lord, make me willing!" What do we love so much today that we are holding onto too tightly? What are we afraid to let God have? What places in our hearts is God asking us for that we have refused Him to let Him have because of fear or denial or even inconvenience?

Needs Met by God Alone

When God takes us into the deep through an "off-the-map" route, He provides for us in powerful and incredible ways. He knows what we need, and He knows how to lead us. This is exactly what happened with the children of Israel in the wilderness. They had a front-row seat as they watched God go before them deep into the wilderness and off the map.

> After leaving Sukkoth they camped at Etham on the edge of the desert. By day the Lord went ahead of them in a pillar of cloud to guide them on their way and by night in a pillar of fire to give them light, so that they could travel by day or night. Neither the pillar of cloud by day nor the pillar of fire by night left its place in front of the people.
>
> **Exodus 13:20–22 (NIV)**

It is such a powerful thing the way God cares for His people. We so easily forget that if He is asking us to follow Him off the map, He will provide for us! He knew the children of Israel needed to travel by day and by night, so He provided for them exactly what they needed in this place: a cloud during the day for shade from the desert sun and a fire by night to warm them and to light up the darkness. More importantly, God gave them a sign of His presence and His protection through the pillar of cloud and of fire. This is how God chose to lead them safely through the desert!

My husband, Paul, and I have been married for over twenty-five years, and God has taken us many times off the map in this area of trusting Him alone to meet our needs! We were married in July 1997, and like most brides, I was so nervous and distracted as we stood there at the altar that I found it difficult to pay attention to anything the pastor was saying to us about marriage. But then he began to read a scripture out of Philippians to us. "And my God will meet all your needs according to the riches of his glory in Christ Jesus" (Philippians 4:19, NIV). Slowly, he reread it. "And my God will meet all of your needs, not some of your needs but all of your needs according to His glorious riches in Christ Jesus." He reread again. "My God WILL supply all of your needs according to His glorious riches in Christ Jesus." I began to focus on what the pastor was saying. I let the words settle deep into my spirit. I knew God was making a mark on my heart. I knew God was speaking to Paul and me through this pastor and through this scripture.

A Lifeline

That was such a prophetic moment for us that day, even though we didn't know it at the time, as we stood there at the altar and joined our lives together. God was giving us a promise from Him that He knew we would need, like a lifeline, in future days. We had been married about five years when we faced the first of three major job layoffs. Like so many others during that time, we found ourselves in the middle of a jolted economy, and the effects of it hit us in a very personal way. Paul and I found ourselves crushed and scared and not understanding the road we were heading down.

Early one morning, as I was just starting my day at work in Birmingham, Alabama, there was a sudden commotion and people rushing into different conference rooms. I realized they were going to turn on the TV. I went to see what was happening for myself. It was Tuesday, September 11, 2001. As we all stood in silence, we went to channel after channel, and each one flashed with breaking news as the unimaginable terror of that day unfolded. I was numb with shock. I watched in agony the pictures and video clips of the horror and the destruction of the inconceivable attacks against our nation. Suddenly, there were scared people all around us! Fear and panic hung in the air like the enormous clouds of dust that rolled through Manhattan that morning when the two Trade Center buildings collapsed. Like so many Americans and others from around the world, I was utterly devastated and outraged at the same time. I could hardly believe what I had just seen. And then the fear began to wash over me in waves.

One night I was very upset and fearful about our future. Paul was out late working at restaurants we used to go to as a parking valet while we were waiting to see where God would lead us next, and I was home alone doing the laundry. I cried out to God to show us the way. I told Him we were in a desperate place and desperately needed to hear from Him! (As if He was totally unaware of what was going on with us or what we needed!) Paul came home that night, and we got down on our knees together and asked God to step in and make a way. We reminded ourselves of what God promised us on our wedding day. "My God WILL supply all of your needs according to His glorious riches in Christ Jesus."

Before all these events happened, we had been sensing that a change was coming for us. We had been looking for ways to be closer to my family in Virginia Beach, but the door always seemed to close when a good opportunity presented itself. That's when it dawned on us that maybe this was, in fact, the route God would use to take us to a new place. Despite the closed doors and all! So, we went and bought a "For Sale" sign, and we stood in our yard and prayed. "God, we don't know what is happening right now, but we are giving you everything," we prayed together. "We give you our home, and if you are sending us out…make the way." God did make the way. After three months of praying and believing, Paul got a call from a great company offering a high-level position that also required a move to Virginia Beach. We literally watched God open the path before us and draw us a new map. It wasn't the map we would have chosen for ourselves, but God was putting strength in our souls and teaching us how to TRUST His provision for us.

Three more times since, we have gone down that same road of job change and job layoffs, and every single time, God has provided everything we needed. He provided homes and land, friends and family, clothes and shoes, and food and health. He has watched over us and has continued to restore everything lost along the way. He has been our pillar of cloud by day and our pillar of fire by night. I know in my heart that we aren't finished with this lesson. There are days yet to come for us when He will ask us to trust Him yet again and allow Him to stretch us beyond what we can see and where the lines of *our* map have been drawn! Most likely, He will be asking us to go get more paper because there is a reroute coming! We will have to remember once again that His track record for us, even in the rough places, has always been FAITHFUL and TRUE. He's not about to fail us now! And He is not about to fail YOU now!

Turn Here

God never takes us into uncharted waters and then leaves us there without the promise of His presence. God knows our every need, just as He understood the needs of the children of Israel when they wandered through the wilderness. He knew that they would need to see where to go, so He became a cloud and a fire for them. He will do the same for us! He knew the children of Israel would need shade from the sun and from the enemy behind them, so He became a cloud of protection. He will do the same for us! He knew they would be hungry and need food, so He provided for them a special food He created that would meet all of their nutrition needs in the desert—manna. He offers the same to us! And when they became bored with the "sameness" of the manna, he brought them quail.

Even though the terrain was rugged and the lessons hard, God never left His children with unmet needs, not even for a single moment. He demonstrated to them the same way that He is willing to demonstrate to you and me today that HE is Jehovah Jireh, the Lord our PROVIDER.

> He humbled you, causing you to hunger and then feeding you with manna, which neither you nor your ancestors had known, to teach you that man does not live on bread alone but on every word that comes from the mouth of the Lord. Your clothes did not wear out and your feet did not swell during these forty years.[…]
>
> For the Lord your God is bringing you into a good land—a land with brooks, streams, and deep springs gushing out into the valleys and hills; a land with wheat and barley, vines and fig trees, pomegranates, olive oil and honey; a land where bread will not be scarce and you will lack nothing; a land where the rocks are iron and you can dig copper out of the hills.

Deuteronomy 8:3–4, 7–9 (NIV)

God creates a need in us so that He can fill it! He wants to be the first place we look for that need to be met. We are challenged when our journey suddenly veers off the map. Part of the challenge is to look to Him, to come to Him and be filled! What areas of our lives do we find ourselves constantly trying to fill with something other than Jesus?

We will always find ourselves in a place of endless want when we don't allow Jesus to be our true Source. Endless want will take us down roads of addiction and obsession with things that can never compare to Jesus. He alone fills every empty place! One of the names of God is El Shaddai, the All-Sufficient One. There is nothing we need that He cannot provide. When all is said and done, Jesus IS all we need. He is the God who IS enough.

The Place Where Supernatural Doors Open

In 1 Corinthians 16, Paul told the church, "A wide door for effective service has opened to me [in Ephesus, a very promising opportunity], and there are many adversaries" (1 Corinthians 16:9, AMP).

He understood the significance of an open door and the "companion" of resistance that would follow it by means of many adversaries! There will always be great resistance to breakthroughs when a supernatural door is opened! But regardless and without fail, doors will open. Why? Because God is true to His Word, and He cannot fail. *We* might fail along the way through times when our hope fades, and our eyes fail while looking for the promise. But God cannot fail. So, at just the right time, He sends His Word, and on the authority of that Word alone, doors open.

These doors are ones we never open for ourselves, and we couldn't even if we tried. Doors of destiny, doors of mission, doors of rescue, and doors of opportunity! We will find ourselves out of our depth and beyond our comfort, in places of influence, in positions of God-given purpose. I love this part of the journey off the map because it is where God walks us from an unknown land into a place of promise. One of the greatest doors God opens to us as we head off the map is His supernatural protection so that we can accomplish what He has called us to do!

Corrie ten Boom

Corrie ten Boom is one of the great heroines of the faith. If you have not read one of her books, you need to do so, especially her book *The Hiding Place*. It is amazing. Corrie ten Boom's father was a watchmaker and owned a small watch shop in Holland during the 1930s and 1940s and during Adolph Hitler's rise to power during the Second World War. The story of the Ten Boom family is both enduring and an inspiration. Like many Dutch families, the Ten Booms were hard-working people who loved each other and loved their country. Corrie's mother died at an early age, and Corrie and her two older sisters and older brother were raised by their father. Mr. ten Boom was a devoted Christian who taught Corrie and her siblings to love Jesus and serve Him with all of their hearts. As things began to deteriorate in Europe, with Hitler gaining more and more power, the persecution of the Jewish people intensified. Germany invaded the Netherlands in 1940 and, with their swift victory, brought their policies to bear upon the Dutch people, including severe restrictions upon the Jews. Corrie and her family, compelled by their faith in God and a love for the Jewish people, began hiding Jews in their modest home located on the second and third stories directly above their small watch shop. They created a hiding place within one of the walls in Corrie's bedroom in order to save as many people as they could. The Ten Boom family became an integral part of the Dutch Underground Resistance during the years of the Nazi occupation. Jewish families would often spend days, sometimes weeks, in the often-crowded living quarters. A large number of Jewish refugees and their families passed through the Ten Boom home as they fled the horrors of the ensuing Nazi Holocaust and made their way into other parts of Europe. And then, in early 1944, the Ten Boom family and their heroic work were exposed by an informer. The entire family was arrested, including a nephew and six people hiding in the secret room. They were sent to Scheveningen Prison, where Corrie's father subsequently died. Remarkably, Corrie's sister, Nollie, and brother, Willem, and the nephew were released from the prison. Corrie and her other sister, Betsie, however, remained imprisoned. Corrie and Betsie managed to stay together when they were transferred to the Vught Prison, a concentration camp for political prisoners, and then on to the Ravensbrück death camp in Germany. Betsie died there within the year at the hands of a ruthless and cruel prison guard.

During their time in prison, God used Corrie and Betsie mightily as they ministered to their fellow inmates. They even ministered to a number of the prison guards. In her books, Corrie ten Boom relates incredible stories of God's power and faithfulness while she was quite literally "off the map." One of these stories is found in her book *Clippings From My Notebook,* where she tells of the protection of the Most High.

> Many people came to know and trust the Lord during World War II. One was an Englishman who was held in a German prison camp for a long period of time. One day he was reading Psalm 91: "He who dwells in the shelter of the Most High Will abide in the shadow of the Almighty. I will say to the Lord, 'My refuge and my fortress, My God, in whom I trust!' For you have made the Lord, my refuge, Even the Most High, your dwelling place. No evil will befall you, Nor will any plague come near your tent. For He will give His angels charge concerning you, To guard you in all your ways."
>
> "Father in Heaven," he prayed, "I see all these men dying around me, one after the other. Will I also have to die here? I am still young and I very much want to work in Your kingdom here on earth." He received this answer: "Rely on what you have just read and go home!" Trusting in the Lord, he got up and walked into the corridor toward the gate. A guard called out, "Prisoner, where are you going?"
>
> "I am under the protection of the Most High," he replied. The guard came to attention and let him pass, for Adolf Hitler was known as "the Most High."
>
> He came to the gate, where a group of guards stood. They commanded him to stop and asked where he was going. "I am under the protection of the Most High." All the guards stood at attention as he walked out the gate. The English officer made his way through the German countryside and eventually reached England, where he told how he had made

his escape. He was the only one to come out of that prison alive.

(Ten Boom 1982)

Nothing can hold back the plans of God for our lives! There is no door that He can't open before us and pave the way! The Bible promises, "What he opens no one can shut, and what he shuts no one can open" (Revelation 3:7, NIV). God IS able!

What doors are you believing God to open in your life right now? Do not stop believing! Continue to pray boldly for open doors as you follow the call of God on your life. Consider what God promised King Cyrus.

> This is what the Lord says to His anointed, to Cyrus [king of Persia], Whose right hand I have held To subdue nations before him, And I will ungird the loins of kings [disarming them]; To open doors before him so that gates will not be shut: "I will go before you and level the mountains; I will shatter the doors of bronze and cut through the bars of iron.

Isaiah 45:1–2 (AMP)

God declared that He opens doors no one can shut. He promised to level mountains and make crooked places straight. He promised to break in pieces doors of bronze and cut iron bars. Remind yourself of these facts as you pray to Him for the door you need to be opened. He is a faithful God.

The safest place to keep our lives is in the center of God's will! The doors He opens are always doors we could never open on our own. How incredible it is to know you can trust God to do the impossible. When you have experienced His faithfulness in one area or in one particular situation, you gain confidence in who God is and what He is capable of doing. These times build our faith for the times yet to come! We store away our victories and save them for evidence of what God has already done to face the next mountain. This confidence enables us to come boldly before Him. And this is where the collision of the supernatural help from God and our natural situation takes place. We become more willing, more inclined to follow Him even into uncharted waters, to places that are off the map. When we do so, we show God that we trust Him to bring us safely to the other side. And that pleases Him.

LAUNCHING POINTS CHAPTER 7

- Is there a place in your own journey right now that you sense God inviting you to go that is "off the map?" Where do you believe He is asking you to go? (It doesn't always mean a location move! He could be asking you to go across the street!)

- What, if anything, do you feel could be keeping you from following Him at this level? Are there areas of comfort that need to be challenged in your life right now? Write down what God speaks to you, and take some time to ask Him to rework the places in your heart that have held you back up until this point.

CHAPTER 8

KEEP THE CHANNEL CLEAR

Channels play a very important function in the seas and oceans around the world. By definition, a channel is a broad strait that connects two seas. For two seas to connect, one feeding life into another, an open channel is critical. You see, it's the channel that allows for the transfer. If the channel isn't clear or if there is even a slight obstruction, it impacts what kind of elements will pass from one body of water through to the other body of water. It will either transfer life-giving elements to the next sea, or if blocked, it can damage the other body of water by starving it of those same life-giving elements. Open channels between bodies of water also allow for harmful elements to pass. This is why it is so important to keep the channel clear and open.

As we journey into the deep and into greater levels of knowing Jesus, this will be one of the most important assignments we will have along the way. Progress! And in order to make progress, our movement and advancement beyond where we are today in our relationship with Jesus are dependent upon us intentionally keeping the channel of our lives clear. It is important for us to keep the right channels clear and to prevent wrong channels from opening to us. Waters that once ran clear can become contaminated with unknown pathogens and evil elements, which transfer all the wrong things.

Just a Little

A while back, I became very sick in bed with an infection that just wouldn't seem to go away. My doctor prescribed an antibiotic he was sure would work to bring the infection in my body under control. After about three days of obediently taking the antibiotic, I woke up early one morning feeling that something wasn't quite right. I went into my bathroom and took one look at my face in the mirror and realized I was in trouble. I was bright red, almost as though I was badly sunburned, and I had an incredibly high fever. As I felt my face, trying to determine what was wrong, the simple touch caused it to burn like fire. To my horror, I then discovered my entire body was covered in this horrible, fiery rash! I felt as though I was on fire. I was in such agony! Paul rushed me to the doctor, where I was immediately evaluated. I was relieved when it was determined that I had had a horrible allergic reaction to the antibiotic that was in my system, as small as the amount was! I was informed that if I *ever* take a medicine again in the future with that ingredient in it, I could literally die! As I learned that day, it doesn't take much of the wrong thing to create a huge problem.

The same thing can happen inside our spirit when even a small amount of pollution enters.

> You were running a good race. Who cut in on you to keep you from obeying the truth? That kind of persuasion does not come from the one who calls you. "A little yeast works through the whole batch of dough." I am confident in the Lord that you will take no other view. The one who is throwing you into

confusion, whoever that may be, will have to pay the penalty.

Galatians 5:7–10 (NIV)

This passage in Galatians reminds us that even the smallest of things can completely change the course of our life. Long before the effects of pollution are seen in an outward way, causing sickness and disease to take over, the pollution has been growing at a microscopic level.

Keeping a free heart and an open spirit is something we do through the help of the Holy Spirit and as an act of our will. When Paul wrote to the churches in the province of Galatia, he asked, "What caused the *progress* of your life to be threatened? Why did you stop obeying what you knew God was telling you to do?" Great questions. Obviously, the Galatian churches were beginning to show the effects of the pollution they had allowed to flow into their midst. These questions are just as valid today as they were when the apostle Paul wrote his letter to the churches in Galatia. What has threatened *your* progress in your walk with Jesus? Have *you* stopped obeying what the Word says to do?

Obedience

I believe one of the greatest pollutants in our spirits that stops us from progressing in God is a lack of obedience. Usually, when disobedience is taking root in us, it starts in small areas and then works its way into larger places of our lives if it is allowed to go unchecked. Disobedience to God always begins with compromise.

Compromise is disobedience in disguise. When we enter into an area of compromise, we hold back an area of our lives from God so that we can do what *we* want to! We reason, we justify, and we make room for "a little sin." Then we make the mistake of thinking it won't pollute our whole lives. We downplay the boundary lines that God has clearly laid out for us when we allow areas of compromise to thrive in our lives. In fact, it does something very serious inside of us. It causes our spirit to become dull. It causes a breakdown in our movement toward God. Proverbs explains it best:

> I passed by the field of a sluggard, by the vineyard of a man lacking sense, and behold, it was all overgrown with thorns; the ground was covered with nettles, and its stone wall was broken down. Then I saw and considered it; I looked and received instruction. A little sleep, a little slumber, a little folding of the hands to rest, and poverty will come upon you like a robber, and want like an armed man.

Proverbs 24:30–34 (ESV)

Compromise opens the door to places of tolerance, allowing tolerance to form in our lives for things that feed our flesh and not our spirit. The above passage in Proverbs illustrates how just a little sleep and a little slumber lead to poverty. The compromise? Laziness. The man identified in this passage obviously was blessed to own a field and to have a vineyard, but he grew lazy and stopped caring for them. He woke up one day and said, "I am too tired this morning to go out to the field or to my vineyard." He compromised. He disobeyed the command to work and to care for his field and vineyard. When he stopped caring for them, they became overgrown with weeds and brush. His fields and vineyards became a mess over time. He tolerated "sleepiness" when he should have been working his field. "Oh, this little nap won't hurt me! I can give myself a break for some 'me' time" Unfortunately, his "me" time turned into "me" *times* and eventually into full-blown laziness. In the end, his whole blessing (the field and vineyard) was affected!

We somehow think we will be able to balance both of these things: serving God and following Him while also doing what we want to do! The above passage from Proverbs serves as a serious cautionary tale about giving even a little bit of room to compromise! A little spiritual sleep, a little less momentum, a little less hunger? It will most certainly open the door to destruction and can be so dangerous to our progress. It doesn't take much!

Rule Your Spirit!

Another way we can open the door to compromise and disobedience is through a lack of self-control! As I have mentioned before in this book, I have two sisters and one brother, and we were all born in the span of five years! Having so many kids so close in age, my parents had to regain control of the "ship" constantly! From a very young age, my mom and dad began to teach us how to have rule over our own spirit so that we could obey when they told us to obey! When we would start to lose it when we were told to do something we didn't want to do, there were no "countdowns" to obedience. There were no long conversations trying to convince us to "like" obeying! I mean, have you ever met a kid that was born loving boundaries and adoring correction? Me either. My mom and dad would calmly (and swiftly!) come to us and say, "Rule your spirit!" In that moment, we knew we had the opportunity to calm down and submit, or we could keep walking down the well-traveled road of the "meltdown." But then we would have to brace ourselves for the immediate consequences! And there *were* consequences!

I have a friend who has five children of her own. As her children were growing up, she and her husband would remind them that the "first form of government is self-government." Then they would tell them to "govern themselves" or expect a "government take-over!"

I might have been young at the time, but I was learning that I *did* and *do* have control over my own spirit! I began to recognize that I did not have to be marched around by my own flesh. (I learned that I really *could* stop crying almost instantly and carrying on as a kid!) When we lack self-control, it stops our progress in God. Our life becomes polluted because we haven't learned the discipline of doing even the simple things that God tells us to do that will keep us moving forward in Him! In 1 Corinthians 9, Paul tells us how important this issue of self-control is to our effectiveness in the work of God.

> Do you not know that in a race all the runners run, but only one gets the prize? Run in such a way as to get the prize. Everyone who competes in the games

goes into strict training. They do it to get a crown that will not last, but we do it to get a crown that will last forever. Therefore I do not run like someone running aimlessly; I do not fight like a boxer beating the air. No, I strike a blow to my body and make it my slave so that after I have preached to others, I myself will not be disqualified for the prize.

1 Corinthians 9:24–27 (NIV)

It is such a sobering thought to think that after all the information we take in, books we read, services we sit in, conferences we attend, as well as all the victories that God brings in our lives to show us His power, we could shipwreck our own progress because we cannot bring ourselves under God's control! The apostle Paul tells us in the passage above that if we live with a lack of self-control, we have an aimless quality to our life! Instead of living with the goal in mind, namely, more of Jesus, we will find that the goalposts begin to move depending on our mood that day.

God will always put His finger on our lack of self-control because, if it is not addressed, He cannot trust that we will have the necessary discipline to press through in the bigger battles that lie ahead! Let me just say right here that this internal battle is one that we will all fight until we go to heaven! As long as we live in the flesh, we will be fighting our flesh! (Remember, our flesh is what *we want,* what *we think*, and what *we feel.*) We tend to give these thoughts way more room to rule over us than we even know! If you are in a battle right now, be encouraged as you press through the pain of obedience in EVERY area of your life that God is on your side. If you ask Him, He will enable you to put the right things in and to keep the wrong things out!

Whatever we feed in our lives is what will grow the largest! We can feed our spirit, which the Bible tells us will show in areas of outward fruit, or we can feed our flesh and from it reap corruption and death. Galatians 5:16–25 in The Message Bible lays out very clearly what will keep us moving forward in God and what stops us dead in our tracks.

> My counsel is this: Live freely, animated and motivated by God's Spirit. Then you won't feed the compulsions of selfishness. For there is a root of sinful self-interest in us that is at odds with a free spirit, just as the free spirit is incompatible with selfishness. These two ways of life are contrary to each other, so that you cannot live at times one way and at times another way according to how you feel on any given day. Why don't you choose to be led by the Spirit and so escape the erratic compulsions of a law-dominated existence?

> It is obvious what kind of life develops out of trying to get your own way all the time: repetitive, loveless, cheap sex; a stinking accumulation of mental and emotional garbage; frenzied and joyless grabs for happiness; trinket gods; magic-show religion; paranoid loneliness; cutthroat competition; all-consuming-yet-never-satisfied wants; a brutal temper; an impotence to love or be loved; divided homes and divided lives; small-minded and lopsided pursuits; the vicious habit of depersonalizing everyone into

a rival; uncontrolled and uncontrollable addictions; ugly parodies of community. I could go on.

[...]

What happens when we live God's way? He brings gifts into our lives, much the same way that fruit appears in an orchard—things like affection for others, exuberance about life, serenity. We develop a willingness to stick with things, a sense of compassion in the heart, and a conviction that a basic holiness permeates things and people. We find ourselves involved in loyal commitments, not needing to force our way in life, able to marshal and direct our energies wisely. [These are good things.]

Galatians 5:16–23 (MSG)

The idea of "feeding" our compulsions or "starving" them is so important in our ability to make progress into deeper waters. As God gives us revelation on the areas of our lives that we have been feeding that we really need to be starving and we obey, we enable the movement toward God to continue in our lives. I encourage you to go back and reread the passage above from Galatians 5 and reflect upon your own life. Are there areas where God has revealed to you that it's time to "starve"? Every time I read that passage, especially from The Message Bible, God shows me places in my heart that need to be brought back under His control.

I was praying a couple of years ago, and I remember the moment exactly when God began to bring up some things in my life that were slipping and needed to be reined in. So, I started to pray that thought through. As I did this, a sentence came out of my mouth that shocked me. I knew it was a Holy Spirit inspired prayer because this sentence isn't one that naturally comes out of our mouths. I began to pray, "God, I give You my appetites. Discipline my appetites. Discipline the areas where I'm beginning to fill up on the wrong things. Take over!" I meant it. It wasn't a quiet prayer. I remember it rising in me! God wanted to redirect my appetite again for HIM in every area, not just some areas. And here's the amazing thing, HE DID IT! I don't know why I was so shocked when my cravings *really* changed, but I was!

Just for clarification, appetites aren't just about food. They also are about what you are hungry for outside of food! Sometimes you don't have an appetite for something, but if you head into a restaurant and begin to smell what they are cooking, you suddenly become hungry for whatever that thing is. While it smells amazing if you eat a little of it, before you know it, that thing is GONE. What you once had no appetite for, *you made room for*, and now you consume it regularly. It has become a habit. We need to be aware of the things the devil might be trying to use against us to change what we crave! Maybe for you it is a craving to be promoted, and it begins to rule you to the point that you cannot be content where you are while you wait. Maybe it is shopping. Maybe it is about position, place, or prominence. The list can go on and on! If left unchecked and undisciplined, over time, the writing is on the wall, and that *very* thing that started so small, so "harmless," will be *the* thing that takes us out.

God can change your motives, your desires, what you think you need, everything. He can change something you used to crave right now into an aversion! It's amazing. If you ask Him, He can help you make the shifts that need to be made in your life right now! No matter what it looks like right now in this area for you, remember that Scripture tells us in Philippians, "I can do all this through him who gives me strength" (Philippians 4:13, NIV). God's power is available to help us do what we cannot do in our own strength!

It's All about the Transfer

As we learned at the outset of this chapter, a channel between two seas has a very important function, *transfer.* It is a point of connection and communication of whatever elements lie within the waters. We can't get away from the power of the transfer in our lives. What is inside of us never affects just us! Who we are always leaks and comes out, and when it does, it transfers to the people around us. If the good fruit that Galatians 5 talks about is present, then that is what we will transfer into the life of another. However, if our lives have become contaminated through areas of tolerance to sin, then that is what our lives will transfer to other people around us!

There is a fascinating story of a devastating cholera outbreak in the 1850s in the Soho district of London, England. Next to the plague, cholera was one of the leading causes of death in Europe at the time. London had already experienced several smaller cholera outbreaks throughout the city and surrounding suburbs, but nothing compared to the outbreak in Soho on August 31, 1854. Within days of the initial outbreak on Broad Street, over a hundred people died. Within the next several weeks, the number of people who died in the immediate area of Broad Street escalated to over six hundred! There was widespread panic.

Medical science was in its infancy at the time. Theories abounded on how cholera was spreading. Many physicians felt that both the cholera disease and the bubonic plague spread as a result of breathing pollution or "foul air," as doubtful as that was. One doctor, John Snow, MD, however, felt differently about the situation. Snow was convinced that the cholera outbreak could be traced to a polluted water supply. His research eventually pinpointed the source to a water pump on Broad Street as the epicenter. It was later determined that the well had been dug in close proximity to an abandoned cesspit, and raw sewage was seeping into the well. People who used the public pump on Broad Street were simply drawing *contaminated* water from a polluted source (Tulchinsky 2018). This story in history illustrates so clearly that *contamination will always spread*!

The Cure is Jesus!

We have a God-given responsibility to spread the message of Jesus and transfer it through our lives and into the lives of those around us. We are not to contaminate the world around us with pollutants that will cause others to stumble. As we seek to be closer to Jesus, the more we will find ourselves challenged to reach out and touch the lives of those with whom we come in contact!

When we realize that we have within our hands the very life and power of God, then we can put that same life and power into the hands of everyone we meet along the way. This is a revelation that I believe God wants for every believer. The revelation that we have been chosen and are responsible for the transfer! As the apostle Paul declares in 2 Corinthians 2:15–16 (NKJV), "For we are to God the fragrance of Christ among those who are being saved and among those who are perishing. To the one we are the aroma of death leading to death, and to the other the aroma of life leading to life."

Our lives, free and clear of pollutants, will smell fresh and clean, not to mention ATTRACTIVE in a world that is lost without Jesus. There is a brightness that begins to emerge in our lives when we remember that every day we hold the keys in our hands to freedom, not just for ourselves, but for another. The heart of God for us is to use our lives in such a way as to cause others to catch a glimpse of Jesus. Paul encouraged believers to live in such a way that others would recognize the light of Jesus in them.

> That you may prove yourselves to be blameless and guileless, innocent and uncontaminated, children of God without blemish in the midst of a [morally] crooked and [spiritually] perverted generation, among whom you are seen as bright lights [beacons shining out clearly] in the world [of darkness].
>
> **Philippians 2:15 (AMP)**

One way we can show ourselves to be blameless and guileless, as Paul encouraged, is to keep the channel of our life clear and open, to keep it free of pollutants from the world's system, attitudes, and culture so that our lives remain innocent and uncontaminated. However, this doesn't mean that we live in a bunker somewhere underground to stay free of spiritual contaminators! Jesus didn't say, "HIDE OUT from all the world!" He told us all to "go INTO all the world!" Through Jesus, it is completely possible to stay CLEAN and live in this world at the same time. Through His blood applied to our lives that cleanses and renews and in the power of the Holy Spirit, we are ABLE! But it will mean ongoing attention, care, and maintenance of our own channels to stay effective in the days to come. No one is immune. I don't care who you are.

This is a work that we will spend our entire lives doing. So, as Revelation 3 tells us, "Strengthen what remains" (Revelations 3:2, NIV). Stay close to Jesus. This is what going into the deep is all about, what it looks like. It is worth every battle to keep moving toward Jesus. As we do, our lives will bear the fruit of obedience and transfer the fragrance of Jesus everywhere we go.

LAUNCHING POINTS CHAPTER 8

- In your life right now, are you experiencing a "halt" in your progress toward the things of God?

- Is there an area that, even as you read this question, you sense God highlighting to you that may be an area of compromise? Take the time to ask God to show you places where you have allowed the little things to come into your life that you know aren't pleasing to Him. Then ask Him to help you keep a heart and spirit that are free to serve Him instead of being weighed down by areas of known sin.

- What are you craving right now? Do you get a tugging in your heart that it is something that needs to have less power over you? Take some time to think and wait on God; ask Him to reveal it to you if you don't know exactly what it is. Then pray for Him to discipline your appetites and take control of your focus again.

- Seek out someone you trust and make yourself accountable to them. Let them help you as you journey further into the deep.

CHAPTER 9

THE MIRACULOUS

He [Jesus] said to them, "Go into all the world and preach the gospel to all creation [...] And these signs will accompany those who believe: In my name they will drive out demons; they will speak in new tongues; they will pick up snakes with their hands; and when they drink deadly poison, it will not hurt them at all; they will place their hands on sick people, and they will get well."

Mark 16:15–18 (NIV)

When we dare to follow Jesus out of the known and into the deep of the unknown, we enter a place where the miraculous occurs. God loves to respond to great faith and total abandonment for those who follow Him into the deep. This is the place in God where literally anything is possible!

Jesus gave simple and straightforward instructions to His disciples before He ascended back to heaven. He told them to go into the world and preach the good news, to tell the world about the love of the Father and all that He (Jesus) had done while on the earth. And He told them that as they preached, signs and wonders would follow! In the book of Mark, it says, "Then the disciples went out and preached everywhere, and the Lord worked with them and confirmed his word by the signs that accompanied it" (Mark 16:20). Jesus was true to His word. Today, we are still living this part of the story! We are living in the "Go into all the world" mission that Jesus defined for the disciples in Mark 16:15–18. What He commissioned them to do is no less than what He has commissioned us to do. We are to go into all the world and preach the good news of the gospel. But we were never meant to stop there! We should fully *expect* the signs and wonders Jesus told His disciples would happen to happen to us, as well! We are not supposed to just fulfill the first part of this scripture while ignoring the signs that Jesus said *will* follow. God wants to move in power through every person who believes in the Lord Jesus Christ! Yet, somehow, we have allowed a separation to take place between the "go into all the world" commission and the "and these signs will accompany." Simply stated, we leave the power at home!

Overcoming the Fear Factor

It's been said that we fear what we don't understand! I think this statement is generally true. Stated another way, there is a fear of the unknown. I believe that this fear of the unknown or the fear stemming from what we don't understand has worked its way into many of the people of God. It has crept into the hearts of many believers and weakened them. As we have spoken about earlier in the book, the fear of the unknown in this area of miracles keeps us from moving in the power of the Holy Spirit. I believe that this is what has caused the real miracle-working power of Jesus to become a rare sight in the Western world especially. This separation of the commission to preach the gospel and the outworking of the power of God has literally divided the church, especially as it concerns speaking in tongues, modern-day prophecy, and with the miraculous.

In chapter 2, "The Prompting," I mentioned that when we learn to hear the voice of God and respond, the devil will do everything in his limited power to stop us. It is important to remember that while the Holy Spirit is speaking, the devil is imitating! To be sure, the devil does not want us speaking in tongues or being empowered by the Holy Spirit. The same is true with the miraculous. When God reveals His genuine power, that power will *always* point to Jesus. And the devil despises anything that points people to Jesus! In some cases, he immediately tries to imitate a real miracle. He uses misguided people and false prophets and preachers to move through and perform his lying wonders. This is part of *why* many Christians want no part in the miraculous. People who make a great effort to draw attention to themselves, use manipulation, or charge money for healings, etc. have done very real damage to the kingdom of heaven in this area. With a lying wonder (or miracle), often the symptoms may subside or even stop temporarily (appearing real) if it involves healing. Other times, a "natural" or "logical" solution presents itself, and the miraculous is reduced to something normal or common.

This is confusing for people who came to genuinely see God move! Some are led to believe that the miracle they just witnessed *was* from God! But there are always indicators that someone is not moving in the Holy Spirit. (Among many red flags God uses to warn us that something isn't right, remember in chapter 2 the conversation about doors. Reread if necessary!) An imposter will always enter through another door than Jesus. The end result is that the devil distorts the miraculous event and uses it to mislead people from turning to Jesus. Leaving them disillusioned and disappointed with God! (Even though He had nothing to do with what just happened!)

Yet another way in which the devil maligns God's miraculous power is when he sows seeds of doubt and unbelief in the hearts of God's people. "God isn't going to come through for you." Or "You're not really healed." So often, this is what a person believing for a miracle hears. The devil is a master deceiver. He will lie and cause confusion and whatever else he can come up with in order to get a person to stop believing what God has promised.

And then, at times, there is the local church. It is amazing how many well-intended people there are in the local churches who have such little understanding of the things of God and the promises found in His Word. While they mean well, they often do more harm than good in this area. Even more amazing is the number of believers who do not believe in the miraculous to begin with and who do what they can to reject the power of God! (Most don't even realize that's what they are doing.) The devil thrives on these negative experiences with people and churches who remain ignorant or mishandle the Word of God. As a result, the "miraculous" is dismissed, and the door is tightly closed on the subject. Why? Many pastors and people are afraid of negative associations!

Words like "emotionalism," "sensationalism," "charismatic," and "flamboyant" surround genuine moves of God, and as a result, it deprives many of what God can do!

As I have stated before, I believe these are important days in which we are living, and God is calling every believer to become fully equipped to demonstrate Jesus to the world. When we shut the door on *anything* we don't understand as it concerns the things of God, we become dangerously limited and stunted in our ability to communicate who He really is and what He really is able to do. When we seek to know Jesus on a deeper level, we stop shutting the door on what God is attempting to do in us and through us. If we don't stop closing Jesus out in the area of the miraculous, it will stop our progress altogether. Keeping an open heart and an open spirit will allow God to demonstrate His power for us and through us for the entire world to see (see Ephesians 1:19).

It's so hard for us as human beings to wrap our heads around the miraculous, unexplainable, or supernatural intervention of God! In fact, many people work overtime to downplay and even disprove the legitimacy of the fact that God can and does move in supernatural ways.

Why Miracles?

I believe that God has used miracles across the ages and still uses them today in every part of the world to show His great power! Our human nature is quick to look for "natural reasons" for everything. Because of this, there are times when God jolts this powerless thinking right out of us. He does something crazy and incredible! He does the miraculous! He does the supernatural! After all, He is all-powerful, and He uses this power to reveal that He IS God!

There is POWER in the name of Jesus! The name of Jesus causes walls to come down and chains to fall off! In the book of Acts, it says, "Salvation is found in no one else, for there is no other name under heaven given to mankind by which we must be saved" (Acts 4:12, NIV). The salvation available to us is not just for the saving of our souls, but it is saving power for any situation that we face! When we realize just how *much* power is in the name of Jesus, we can bring it boldly into any situation we face. God uses miracles, signs, and wonders in order to deepen our faith in His ability to bring deliverance! Not only is God able to bring deliverance, but He also uses the miraculous to remind us that He is always present and with us!

When I was in the third grade, my little sister, Corrie, and I were walking home from the bus stop one day after school. It was a foggy afternoon, and I remember it being very difficult to see our street. As we were walking, suddenly, a large, mean dog bolted out of nowhere and charged straight for us! Screaming and scared to death, Corrie and I started to run for home. And then I remembered we had been taught that we could say the name of Jesus, and the devil would have to flee! So, we stopped running and turned around and tried it! We shouted at that mean dog, "In the name of Jesus, we command you to GO away from us!" IT WORKED!

The dog skidded to an abrupt stop, lost interest in us, and then went away! Corrie and I looked at each other like, "Wow! *It really does work!*" I have never forgotten that story because it showed me at a very young age that there is great power and authority in the name of Jesus. We are too quick to shrink under the onslaught of attacks that come against us. In doing so, we give power to the attack instead of taking the authority in the NAME of Jesus and coming against it! We yield when we should wield! We yield to the attack when we should wield the authority that has been given to us!

In many places around the world, the name of Jesus and all that His name represents is appearing less and less. It is politically incorrect to speak the name of Jesus or use Jesus' name in settings where other beliefs might be present. It is unacceptable to speak the name of Jesus openly unless you include the names of the other gods people might identify with. The devil knows of the power and of the authority that the name of Jesus brings to any situation.

He knows that just saying Jesus' name unleashes ALL the power of the LIVING GOD! The name of Jesus is victory, and demons MUST flee! Because he knows this to be true, he deceptively and systematically removes it from as many places as possible! He may be the devil, but he is no dummy. When we bring the name of Jesus into any situation, we immediately take authority over the situation, and the power of darkness is broken. The ability to see the miraculous starts with taking authority, and no authority can be taken until the name of Jesus is called upon!

In an earlier chapter of this book, I told the story of spending time in Indonesia with those courageous pastors. While I was there, they took me on a brief tour of the compound where the whole foundation is headquartered. He shared with me the story of how they were able to acquire the beautiful property where the ministry organization he and his wife started is located.

The pastor and his wife had been praying for a place to meet and offices where they would be able to work. He told of how they were having trouble finding a place that would meet their needs and the needs of this ministry. Property and buildings represented such a massive expense for them! He said that despite that fact, they prayed and asked God to show them the right building and to provide a way to pay for it. Working with a broker, they looked at a number of possibilities. Finally, the broker said, "Well, there is one more place I could show you, but I have shown it to many people, and no one will buy it! We believe evil spirits live in this compound, and people are afraid to go in!" As a result, this particular property had stood empty! Indonesia is a country that has a long history of involvement in witchcraft, pagan religions, and the worship of millions of gods. Consequently, there is a lot of demonic spiritual activity happening at any given time!

The pastors went to see the property. They smiled and said, "We will take it!" After he committed to buying the building, the pastor brought his staff and leaders in to pray over the entire property. They took communion and began to pray powerfully in the name of Jesus. As they were thanking and praising God for the blood of Jesus shed on the cross, the many drinking glasses that had been sitting on a table in the front of the room suddenly burst and exploded! The demonic presence that had set up camp in that place was immediately broken on the authority of the name of the Lord Jesus Christ! God used even the need for a building to showcase His power as the one true God!

This couple and their newly formed foundation were able to buy this property, complete with a compound of buildings (not just one building), at a fraction of the original price because the owners and brokers alike were afraid of the power that they feared lived in that place! The most wonderful part of this story is the way God met the needs of His own people and worked a miracle that would both increase the faith of those who believed and, at the same time, give those who didn't believe an encounter with the LIVING God!

You see, no power can stand against the name of Jesus. At the name of Jesus, the devil MUST FLEE! When we pray in the name of Jesus, every barrier and hindrance to what God can do is removed! Isaiah 10 says, "And it shall come to pass in that day That his burden will be taken away from your shoulder, And his yoke from your neck, And the yoke will be destroyed because of the anointing" (Isaiah 10:27, NKJV). The word "yoke" represents slavery or being bound. A yoke is the large wooden beam that is placed upon the shoulders of an ox in order to control them. Isaiah is announcing that it is the anointing that comes with the presence of God that breaks demonic power and all things that bind and try to control us! This anointing is released when we declare the name of Jesus! God wants to use the anointing that He has placed on every believer to set the captives free. He wants to use you, and He wants to use me (see Isaiah 61 yet again)! There is an anointing (God's enabling power) on our lives to move in the miraculous power of God as part of our inheritance. This is not something that is reserved for pastors only or evangelists alone! This power is for every single one of us who believes in Jesus! If we will only take it…

Right Conditions

While there is no formula for the miraculous, there are certain conditions that tend to be present when God shows up in power. Let me say that again. There is NO formula. If there was a formula, please believe we would try to take the credit for our good use of it! Instead, we rely on Jesus to show up *how* He wants to, *when* He wants to, and *where* He wants to! The miracle is always HIS alone. I love the simplicity of my own experience as a child speaking out the name of Jesus to make a wild dog go away because it reminds me to keep it simple in my approach to the miraculous! The Bible tells us, "'Not by might nor by power, but by my Spirit,' says the Lord Almighty" (Zechariah 4:1, NIV). Let's drill down further here; this scripture is saying this miracle God is about to perform will have nothing to do with my religious or natural effort! It will be done by the Spirit of God. It reminds me that all I need to do is to speak the name of Jesus in order to bring *Him* onto the scene. I don't need to agonize and overthink what the right conditions for a miracle to occur will be; I just need the name of Jesus!

It is so easy to make something complicated that God never intended it to be complicated. We do this when we try to rely on our intellect and our methods. The power of God has never been and will never be contained by a method! So, the first condition for a miracle will involve getting our intellect out of the way and letting go of any sort of human methods (or traditions) we have been clinging to so that God can move. When *we* get out of the way, it releases God to move and gives Him room to do whatever He wants to in the moment. Keep in mind that "moving out of the way" does not mean that we become uninvolved in the miracle process! We stay involved by bringing our faith into the moment!

Faith

The element of faith always brings a response from heaven. When we bring our total belief in Jesus into a situation, and we add it to the total ability of God, something supernatural always happens! In Luke 7, the story of the centurion is just such an example. This particular centurion had a servant, and the servant was greatly loved by the centurion but was sick and about to die. The centurion, having heard about Jesus, sends word to where Jesus was ministering, and instead of requiring Jesus to come into his home to heal the servant (which he could have done as a Roman soldier), the centurion simply said, "Lord, [...] say the word and my servant will be healed" (Luke 7:6–7, NIV). The centurion was so convinced Jesus could heal the dying servant that he said, "Just speak it, and it will be done!" Jesus was moved by this man's faith. In verse 9, Jesus responds, "When Jesus heard this, he was amazed at him, and turning to the crowd following him, he said, 'I tell you, I have not found such great faith even in Israel'" (Luke 7:9, NIV). That servant was healed that day, but Jesus was *moved* by the centurion's great faith. Faith leaves room for God to meet the need in whatever way He chooses. *Our* job is to *believe,* and it is *God's* job to do the work!

I'm absolutely convinced that God wants us to believe Him at greater levels and walk the situations of our lives right up to the line while trusting Him all the way. It is so important to remember, however, that our faith is never in the miracle itself; it is in the lordship of Jesus Christ. Because of this fact, there is no such thing as a failed miracle! God cannot fail (see Malachi 3:6).

True faith trusts God's goodness no matter the outcome. In the book of Daniel, three righteous men faced death when they stood up to the wicked King Nebuchadnezzar by refusing to bow before a golden image the king had created. The king then commanded the entire kingdom to bow down before the idol! The three righteous men responded as follows:

> King Nebuchadnezzar, we do not need to defend ourselves before you in this matter. If we are thrown into the blazing furnace, the God we serve is able to deliver us from it, and he will deliver us from your Majesty's hand. But even if he does not, we want you to know, Your Majesty, that we will not serve your gods or worship the image of gold you have set up.

Daniel 3:16–18 (NIV)

I can imagine that these three righteous men were hoping God would move differently from how they were praying, but that did not change their defiant faith in that moment! Fire or not, they trusted God to deliver them. And they were! After they had been thrown into the fire! They were powerfully delivered that day by a miracle of God even as they were prepared to walk their faith right up to the line and through the fire, regardless of the outcome! Going back to the subject of doubt for a minute, I believe when God wants to bring us out of a doubting place and into a believing place, there is a thought He loves to respond to. It is the same one that Jonathan had for his armor-bearer as they were about to go into dangerous enemy territory when they were in a rock and a hard place: "Jonathan said to his young armor-bearer, 'Come, let's go over to the outpost of those uncircumcised men. Perhaps the Lord will act in our behalf. Nothing can hinder the Lord from saving, whether by many or by few'" (1 Samuel 14:6, NIV).

I believe God wants to put this spirit inside of every one of us. A "perhaps the Lord" spirit! The kind of spirit that BELIEVES that God is able no matter what! We are too quick to come up with reasons why God probably won't heal, probably won't raise the dead, probably won't come through for us! So, we stop asking for God to work miracles in and through our lives.

Perhaps the Lord!

As we are beginning to develop more faith for miracles, there is a way to position our minds that brings the victory of God every time! What if God *does* heal me? What if God *will* bring me provision when I need it? What if God *will* turn my marriage around again? What if God brings me favor? What if He does? Perhaps the Lord! Nothing can hinder the Lord from saving. God wants to put this dare-to-believe spirit in our hearts as we look for Him to act on our behalf!

Another one of the conditions Jesus used to work miracles was when He was in the presence of genuine need. He was always moved with compassion by the people with whom He came into contact. Their need generated His compassion.

> Jesus left the synagogue and went to the home of Simon. Now Simon's mother-in-law was suffering from a high fever, and they asked Jesus to help her. So He bent over her and rebuked the fever, and it left her. She got up at once and began to wait on them. At sunset, the people brought to Jesus all who had various kinds of sickness, and laying his hands on each one, he healed them. Moreover, demons came out of many people, shouting, "You are the Son of God!" But he rebuked them and would not allow them to speak, because they knew he was the Messiah.

> **Luke 4:38–41 (NIV)**

Jesus saw human need as an opportunity to demonstrate the goodness of God by bringing healing and freedom. These are always the motivation behind the miraculous: love, compassion, healing, and freedom! Because of this, we can be confident if there is a need present, Jesus wants to meet it! When we know that this is how He works, we don't have to ask Him *if* it's His will or not.

It IS His will for us to come and ask boldly! *We ask, and then we surrender what that looks like to Jesus.* But never stop asking! We can pray with strength and declare the authority of Jesus' name over the need and have confidence we are in line with His Word. Then we can believe that He will answer the need! My younger sister, Corrie, went on the mission field to Kijabe, Kenya, a few years back to do medical missions work. She was working alongside a pediatric surgeon. They spent a year in Kenya working in the local hospitals and clinics. Corrie had her one-year-old little girl (Alaina) with her during this time. Every morning, after they had dressed for the day, Corrie would take Alaina with her to go into the hospital wards where there were sick women and children and pray over them.

During this time, my sister was also newly pregnant and started to experience severe morning sickness. Corrie was getting more concerned because it was starting to affect her ability to go into the hospital to minister to the sick women and children there! The smell of urine and sickness was so overwhelming that she would often become sick herself! One morning, Corrie dressed Alaina, and together they headed down to the hospital. She said, "I stood outside the hospital and prayed: 'Lord, there is a need in this hospital, and you have called me to go in and meet it. I keep getting sick every time I go in, so I pray in the name of Jesus that you would take away my sense of smell so that I can minister to these women and children freely.'" WHAT A BOLD PRAYER! Corrie said that after she prayed, she walked through the doors of that hospital and literally smelled NOTHING! As soon as she walked out of the hospital, her sense of smell would return. This continued to happen every day until the morning sickness went away! MIRACULOUS!

Wrong Conditions

Just as conditions can be right for a move of God, there can be conditions in place that will prevent a move of God! There is nothing that will quench the atmosphere for the miraculous quicker than an unbelieving, closed-off spirit! A spirit that stiffens when the word "supernatural" or "miracle" is even mentioned. An unbelieving spirit rejects evidence of the power of God altogether. Because there is a lack of belief in the miracle-working power of Jesus, there is a danger to a "familiar" approach to the presence of God, treating it as common or dismissing it as of little value.

Sometimes it's not only unbelief at work; there are times when offense with God is in play as well! I've talked to many people who have told me that *they* have prayed and believed, and "it didn't work!" If this is something that you struggle with as you try to be open to miracles, let me encourage you that there is an important component to *believing* that we cannot forget. We believe for the impossible because "PERHAPS THE LORD" will act on our behalf! But the stance that keeps our hearts from becoming offended at *how* God chooses to heal or deliver is His decision alone. It does NOT mean that He didn't hear our prayer. It means He has a plan that we might not yet understand or see. But the moment we pray, He HEARS. An important confession to make on our part as we ask, and that shuts down the enemy's plan to cause us to become offended, is something like, "God, this is what we are standing on and believing for, YET NOT MY WILL, BUT YOURS BE DONE. We TRUST you regardless of what is ahead!"

It is not unbelief to surrender the ultimate outcome to Jesus. I do want to say, if this is a sharp wound for you, Jesus loves you. He knows right where you are at this very moment, and He is NOT mad at you because of what you feel. His heart is toward you with deep compassion. I believe He wants to restore your faith and give you greater insight about the way He moves and replace that deep offense with His PEACE. You are in good company. There are many times when we all have questions and don't understand what God is doing. A word of love and warning here, be careful about WHO you allow to speak into your life about the miraculous. There are, unfortunately, very misleading, legalistic believers out there who may try to tell you things like, "You just didn't have enough faith for your miracle! That's why it didn't happen!" Or they may say something like, "God couldn't come through for you because there is SIN in your life! He is punishing you!" Well, if that were true, God would do no miracles for ANYONE! We are ALL sinners (Romans 8:28). I'm so glad to tell you that these statements are NOT FOUNDED IN SCRIPTURE! You won't find them in the Word, and they don't match up with WHO Jesus even is! These are *lies,* and it is vital that you *get away* from any spiritual leader, church, or voice that teaches these things or speaks these things to you. They do much damage in people's lives. This is NOT how miracles work!

If you need to talk about the false teaching you have received along the way, feel free to reach out to me or to someone you trust that believes the ACCURATE Word of God! Allow someone trusted to come alongside you and help you UNLEARN bad teaching and RELEARN truth! But whatever you do, don't allow that offense to take root and steal the truth about Jesus from you. Talk to Him; tell Him what you are feeling. Allow Him the chance to bring His power back to life in you again. On the other hand, unbelief altogether will take the possible out of play! This is exactly what happened in Jesus' hometown! Read the account in the book of Mark 6.

> Jesus left there and went to his hometown, accompanied by his disciples. When the Sabbath came, he began to teach in the synagogue, and many who heard him were amazed. "Where did this man get these things?" they asked. "What's this wisdom that has been given him? What are these remarkable miracles he is performing? Isn't this the carpenter? Isn't this Mary's son and the brother of James, Joseph, Judas and Simon? Aren't his sisters here with us?" And they took offense at him.
>
> Jesus said to them, "A prophet is not without honor except in his own town, among his relatives and in his own home." *He could not do any miracles there,* except lay his hands on a few sick people and heal them. He was amazed at their lack of faith.
>
> **Mark 6:1–6 (NIV)**

To me, this is one of the most tragic stories in the whole New Testament. Jesus had already performed many incredible miracles. He had calmed the storm in Mark 4 and delivered the man who was filled with the legion of demons, bound in chains, and banished to a cave somewhere in the region of an area known as the Gerasenes in Mark 5. He also healed the woman with the issue of blood and raised Jairus' daughter from the dead. And by this time, He had already preached to hundreds and thousands of people, and thousands of people had been delivered and healed and set free.

And then Jesus returns to His own hometown. That's where chapter 6 begins. This is where Jesus was raised as a child. This is where His family lived. And on a particular Sabbath day, Jesus entered the synagogue and began to teach. The people were astonished! "Where has this man learned such things, and what wisdom is this?" (Mark 6:2). And then they stopped. "Wait a minute," they said. "Isn't this the carpenter, the son of Mary, the brother of James, John, Judas, and Simon?" "Didn't his sisters live here in town?" (Mark 6:3).

And the people were offended by Him. The people disregarded Jesus and were indifferent to what He was doing because they knew Him. It was no big deal. He was no big deal! After all, they knew Mary and Jesus' family. They lived in the same town together. There was nothing special about Jesus to these people. As far as they were concerned, He was one of them. And one of the most tragic verses in the New Testament reads, "He could not do any miracles there, except lay his hands on a few sick people and heal them" (Mark 6:5, NIV). Incredible! Even Jesus was shocked at their unbelief in verse 6! Everywhere Jesus went, He healed and delivered people. But when He showed up in His own hometown, He could only heal a few people.

Why? Because they did not esteem Jesus for who He was— God in the flesh! The same Jesus who walked into other towns and villages and healed everyone can do nothing at HOME. And the only difference between the towns where everyone was healed and Jesus' hometown, where only a few were healed, centers on their *unbelief.* An unbelieving spirit will always shut down the work of God and bring the supernatural down to the level of human understanding! It is so amazing that out of all the things that caused a complete halt in Jesus' ability to move was a spirit of unbelief! The Creator of the universe walked into their town, and they did not believe. Tragic. Another condition that will prevent the miraculous in our lives is a despising spirit. A despising spirit treats with contempt the genuine miracles of God! It is a heart that is repulsed by the supernatural. Consider the people in the synagogue that Sabbath day when Jesus walked into His hometown. They marveled at His teaching. But when they realized who Jesus was and that they knew His family, they were "offended." They held Jesus in contempt. Unfortunately, there are many circles of Christians that are, in fact, operating in the same way; they despise the miraculous.

When we despise something because we don't understand it, we criticize and reject it. A critical spirit will create barrenness in our lives if we let it continue! There will be an emptiness inside of us when we reject something that God is doing just because we don't understand it. If there have been places of your heart that you have closed off because of a negative church experience, false teaching, or fear and unbelief, I want to encourage you today that Jesus is giving you greater insight into who He is and that you can reopen your heart to Him and trust Him in the area of the miraculous and the supernatural. Jesus said the following of us all:

> Believe me when I say that I am in the Father and the Father is in me; or at least believe on the evidence of the works themselves. Very truly I tell you, whoever believes in me will do the works I have been doing, and they will do even greater things than these, because I am going to the Father. And I will do whatever you ask in my name, so that the Father may be glorified in the Son. You may ask me for *anything* in my name, and I will do it.

John 14:11–14 (NIV)

Friends, Jesus is working miracles every single day on the earth through His people. His promise in this passage says that we will do EVEN GREATER things than the things written about in the Bible! Do you believe that? Think about the many incredible things that took place in the New Testament. Those miracles and supernatural encounters did not end there. They are still happening today. Dare to believe. Dare to step out. Dare to go deeper. We have so much to look forward to. Why? Because we can ask God for anything in the name of Jesus Christ our Lord, and He will do it!

A Word of Warning

As we wrap up this chapter on the miraculous, I sense a responsibility on my part to caution you on a couple of things. I believe there is a genuine stirring happening in our hearts again all over the world for more faith to see the power of God at work. And this is wonderful! But keep watch over your own soul as you seek to see God move in greater ways in the days to come. Specifically, don't become confused and start chasing after seeing the power for power's sake! Don't start following human evangelists, prophets, and pastors from town to town enamored by the "show." (Even if they are good and solid people. And if they are, they won't want you to!) The focus can shift very quickly within our human nature to attach a work of God to a person! Things get muddy when we start admiring and idolizing the people who God is moving *through*! Keep in mind that whenever God moves, it *is* spectacular the way He sweeps through a meeting or a room! But the danger is becoming addicted to and only looking for the miraculous in the eye-catching experience and losing the wonder of the Savior Himself! (Chasing the experience.)

Watch out if your focus shifts to only wanting to see more and more miracles in an extravagant display over a hunger to hear the Word preached and being drawn to Jesus for who HE is. (A symptom of this can look like becoming annoyed with your pastor for moving the meeting forward into a time of opening the Word instead of every meeting being a miracle meeting!) I'm always concerned if I am in a church or service where the Word is *regu-*

larly "skipped" for only a miracle service. If the Word isn't given the time and attention it needs to help us root what we are seeing in the Bible, it won't be long until something goes "off." Mark my words.

We are heading out of balance when the miraculous becomes more important, and any other aspect of knowing Jesus fades into the background! Don't miss the mark by chasing after a "show" atmosphere. God is not a *performer*. That's interestingly NOT one of the many names of God! He didn't send Jesus to earth to perform a "show" or put on an "act" for us! He sent Jesus to save the world and to give us eternity. He sent Jesus to personally reveal Himself to each individual person on the planet in a *way* they can understand! *Genuine* miracles aren't given for the entertainment benefit of those who come to see what's happening. In fact, PROOF that God performed a miracle *isn't even found* in whether it looked breathtaking to us or not! God moves in all sorts of ways. In the simple *and* the breathtaking alike. Sometimes He works instantly; other times, a miracle happens over time! One way is not more important or legitimate than the other. Remember, God decides *how* He will work! Genuine miracles will bring ALL focus, attention, and glory to the MIRACLE WORKER, who is JESUS and not the miracle itself.

LAUNCHING POINTS CHAPTER 9

After reading chapter 9, how did it make you feel when discussing the miraculous? How would you best describe your reaction to miracles and the supernatural? Consider the list below and select the one that best identifies where you are right now as it concerns God's ability to move in this way.

- Believing

- Open

- Closed

- Uncomfortable

- Critical

- Despising

- Unbelieving

- Total rejection

- Never thought about it before!

Take a few minutes to think about where you are right now based on what you selected. Think on why you feel this way about the miraculous. Are you critical or unbelieving? Why? Are you open? Wherever you are on the continuum, allow the Holy Spirit to help you locate where you are and why. Write down your answer. God isn't judging you for whatever your honest answer is! Pray and tell God where you are and why. (His desire is to give you more of Himself). Then ask Him to help you if there might be a need for a change in your heart. Ask Him to search your heart, and then allow Him to do just that. Ask Him for a surge of faith for miracles. God wants to move in your life today!

CHAPTER 10

THE GOAL IS JESUS

The journey into the deep has only one destination, one purpose, and only one goal, and that is more of *Jesus*. The secrets revealed on this journey and every lesson learned along the way all lead us to one place, and that is to be so close to His heart that we would actually begin to look just like Him! This way, when people see us, they see Jesus. That's the goal! And it is all *about* and all *for* Him. He is our greatest reward!

> At one time all these things were important to me. But because of Christ, I decided that they are worth nothing. Not only these things, but now I think that all things are worth nothing compared with the greatness of knowing Christ Jesus my Lord. Because of Christ, I lost all these things, and now I know that they are all worthless trash. All I want now is Christ.
>
> **Philippians 3:7–8 (ERV)**

It is quite a statement to say that nothing compares to Jesus. To have had it all and lost it all and come to this revelation that everything is worthless trash when compared to Jesus. What about for you?

Are We There Yet?

If we are honest, our primary reasons for embarking upon

a journey into the deep can start out with other destinations in mind. Maybe we hit rock bottom and needed a way out. Maybe we know someone who already knows Jesus, and we want what they seem to have. We can desire more peace, more wholeness, greater knowledge, and power! We can be healed and restored. But these are simply benefits. They were never meant to be the goal. As we have learned, there are great benefits to launching out into a deeper place with Jesus.

Regardless of what made you decide to go further into the deeper places spiritually in the first place, the goal must always be to know Jesus. Otherwise, nothing written on the pages of this book will ever actually be able to work in your life! This book will be of little value and will have little effect on your personal walk with God. When Paul was writing his letter to the Philippians, he was in Rome and imprisoned for the first time there. He was essentially living under house arrest, a privilege to which he was entitled as a Roman citizen awaiting trial and the favor he had found with several Roman officials. He was bound in chains and under constant guard while confined to a small, modest house— one which he rented with his own money. He had been reduced to nearly nothing as he poured out his life for the various churches he had started throughout Macedonia. Arrested in Jerusalem on trumped-up charges and denied a trial in a reasonable amount of time, Paul appealed his case to be heard by Caesar. The goal of Paul's life had changed. He realized the things that once held so much importance to him were worth nothing compared to really KNOWING JESUS!

What's My Reward?

We have a preoccupation in our world with being rewarded! We love the thought of being recognized and honored. We love plaques and "certificates of achievement" to make sure others *know* what we have accomplished, even for the tiniest of accomplishments! And if you have ever been to any kind of competition involving children in recent years, you probably noticed that *everyone* gets a trophy—including the losing team! After all, "it's not fair that only the winners are recognized." Why? Because "we are all winners!" Yes, you matter. Yes, God sees you as a winner. But did you win the game? No. No, you didn't. You lost. Go congratulate the person who won and have a seat! Why is that so hard for our culture? What is it inside of us that craves all of the focus, appreciation, and applause that comes from others? Somehow, we believe that we are entitled to a reward or a position or place of prominence, even if it is for showing up for a game and losing! We love the sound of the cheering and applause when our name is called, and we rise to the "stage" to be honored! It seems as if the true meaning of the word "achievement" is in danger of being lost in our politically correct society.

As a result, we have trained ourselves to seek and crave approval from others, and our self-worth has suddenly become based upon external rewards. We have convinced ourselves that unless someone *sees* what we have done and places value on it, then it doesn't matter and isn't important! There is, of course, social media, which can be used for much good, but in this area, it helps nothing! Post something, even something totally inane, and you are rewarded with an instant "like." And who doesn't like that? Paul was saying in the above scripture that he realized that there used to be a number of things that he considered important that no longer held that same value. In fact, they ended up not mattering at all! Imprisoned in Rome, with everything stripped away, Paul had a revelation: nothing matters but Jesus. In the same way, as we near the end of our lives, there is actually very little gray left about what really matters. End-of-life conversations always prove this to be true.

What Really Matters

It has now been several years since I sat with my beautiful Nana in the hospital as she was facing her final days here on earth. She was ninety-two years old and ready to go to heaven. She was sharp in body and mind and strong in spirit right up until the end of her life, so we were able to have some wonderful conversations in the final weeks before she died. "You know, Bethy," she said to me one afternoon, "a lot of what you think matters right now in life and holds such constant importance to you really won't matter anymore when you are this close to heaven!" When she drifted off to sleep, I sat there for a long time and thought about what she said and considered my own life. What had my own goals become?

It is so easy to run around all the time and get caught up with the constant demands of living life that we lose perspective on what really matters. We may even be involved in some truly mean-ingful activities that are really impacting people's lives. When suddenly, we look up and realize that along the way, the goalpost of our life has moved! Is my goal—my reward—feeling significant or feeling important? Is that my goal? Is my reward knowing that what I am doing is having an impact? Is my reward my position or my title? Is my reward my financial success? Is my reward the approval of others? Is this my great reward?

As I sat there next to Nana's hospital bed, I had to answer honestly that, on some levels, the answer was "yes" to these questions. I had allowed some things in my life to mean way too much to my soul. If my reward becomes anything other than Jesus, my soul will never be satisfied with it, no matter how great it is!

Exceeding and Great Reward

God spoke with Abram about this very thing when He came to him and made a covenant with him. "After this, the word of the Lord came to Abram in a vision: 'Do not be afraid, Abram. I am your shield, your very great reward.' But Abram said, 'Sovereign Lord, what can you give me since I remain childless and the one who will inherit my estate is Eliezer of Damascus?'" (Genesis 15:1–2, NIV).

I read this passage; I am always amazed by Abram. Not only does the God of heaven speak to Abram directly, but God even identifies Himself as Abram's exceedingly great reward. As if that was not enough, Abram then has the nerve to ask God for something more! *Really?* God just declared to Abram that He was Abram's exceedingly great reward. Not just any reward. A surpassing-all-other-gifts gift! The God of heaven and earth! Abram didn't get it. And sometimes, we don't either. But God is so good! Full of love and promise for Abram, God gives him what he asks for and then some. And here is some great news! God will do the same for us and gives us, at times, the things we desire because He loves us. Yet, when God offers us Himself in the form of His Son, we don't think it is enough. We pray for everything else before we ask for more of Jesus.

More Than Enough

Jesus wants us to be so filled with Him that we don't *need* any other reward. He wants us so filled with Him that we aren't constantly dissatisfied with our lives but fully satisfied with Him and Him alone. In Psalm 17, David wanted this type of satisfaction.

> By your hand save me from such people, Lord, from those of this world whose reward is in this life. May what you have stored up for the wicked fill their bellies; may their children gorge themselves on it, and may there be leftovers for their little ones. As for me, I will be vindicated and will see your face; when I awake, I will be satisfied with seeing your likeness.

Psalm 17:14–15 (NIV)

There is a natural hunger inside every person's heart for earthly rewards and praise. This hunger or longing never goes away. Some try to stop their hunger with earthly things. They work hard to amass as many material possessions as they can. Yet, no matter how many houses they buy and how many vintage or luxury cars they buy, or how many possessions they acquire, it is never enough.

Others try to numb the hunger inside with all kinds of substances and addictions. The drug problem in this country has now gone so much further than just illegal drug use, as we are all painfully aware of. The medical world reports an unprecedented increase in the dependency on prescription drugs. Doctors are literally bombarded by patients who have need of painkillers and other drugs. There is an insatiable need in our society for *anything* that will dull internal pain. Even if we know this in our head, our needs become so great that we give in to that vice if it promises even a moment of relief or distraction. But there are not enough drugs, alcohol, sex, or STUFF to ever drown out the emptiness found deep inside the soul of one who is broken. The desire to be filled never goes away. The emptiness will remain until there is a realization that nothing on this earth—people, money, power, fame, shopping, drugs, or alcohol—can ever fully satisfy the desperate longing in our souls. The longing and emptiness are real, to be sure. The hole in a person's soul needs to be filled. This filling will never come through earthly means. Jesus is the only One who can fully satisfy the longings we all experience. I just want to say, if you are reading this and are feeling defeated in some area we've just spoken about, there IS hope! There is NO shame in realizing something needs to be broken off your life. Jesus can set you free, and He wants to. He doesn't want you to live in a cycle of addiction and emptiness.

If you realize you need help in some way and that your past efforts to be free haven't "worked," please allow someone to step in and work alongside you. Allow a trained professional to help you get insight on whatever the root of it is inside of you that keeps you in this cycle. The addictions we battle are only symptoms of a greater issue...the root. We can't break a symptom until we deal with the root of the problem. Don't ever give up. Jesus will set you free. Take whatever steps you need to, trust the process, and come out into a NEW season. This is what David understood. He knew that nothing on this earth compared with seeing the face of God. He knew he would only be satisfied in seeing God's likeness. David's realization was, "God, I don't need any other reward! YOU are my greatest reward!"

We, too, must come to that same realization. We need to have the same hunger and desire David had for God's presence. I love what David wrote in Psalm 42:1 (NIV): "As the deer pants for streams of water, so my soul pants for you, my God." What a perfect picture. In the natural, animals that are panting have reached a critical point, especially deer, as it relates to the need for water. There is an instinctive reaction to thirst. In the same way, David trained his soul to crave God alone, to have an appetite that could only be filled by Him. And what's more unbelievable is that Jesus longs for us in the same way! He literally "pants" for us! He wants to give us more of Himself than we have ever had before! It happens when we drop the need for earthly reward, earthly admiration, earthly fame, and importance, and we realize that the greatest reward of all is to truly know Jesus.

THE GOAL IS JESUS

To Be Found in Him

Paul had really discovered the true purpose of his own life when he wrote his letter to the Philippians. He wrote these very life-defining words: "That I may gain Christ and be found in him, not having a righteousness of my own that comes from the law, but that which is through faith in Christ—the righteousness that comes from God on the basis of faith" (Philippians 3:8–9, NIV). When the goal is Jesus, our heart's desire is to be found in Him. The very words that Paul used to define his whole life's meaning and purpose should become the words we desire to use in defining the meaning of our lives. This desire will cause us to have a reaction! That reaction to our heart's desire means that we will want to live every single day of this life with an awareness that we are saved and set free through the power of the cross. Never forgetting the finished work of Jesus Christ, who died for us. We need to realize that the same power that raised Christ Jesus from the dead dwells in us (cf. Romans 8:11) and gives our life strength to live through faith and not by our own strength alone.

This is the place where we choose to position our lives. To be so close to Jesus. Never allowing our lives to have a split purpose of trying to please the world while attempting to stay "in Jesus." Something will have to give. But what does that really mean—to be "in Jesus?" What does that even look like? Here's what Jesus said in John 15:

> Remain in me, as I also remain in you. No branch can bear fruit by itself; it must remain in the vine. Neither can you bear fruit unless you remain in me.

"I am the vine; you are the branches. If you remain in me and I in you, you will bear much fruit; apart from me you can do nothing."

John 15:4–5 (NIV)

So, what does it mean to "stay" in Jesus? It means we are to "remain." In the same way that a branch cannot thrive and bear fruit by itself, we cannot thrive and bear fruit in our lives apart from the True Vine. The branch cannot "decide" to leave the vine. The growth process only works when the branch and the vine are connected. The word "remain" is so important because it implies that one could potentially leave! And so we have a choice. We can either remain or leave. In other words, Jesus is saying in these verses, "When presented with an option to do your own thing and go your own way, STOP! Stay right where you are! Do exactly what I told you to do if you want to have the life I told you could have!" Doing our lives apart from the strength of God will prevent us from growing and cause us to be unfruitful.

You may be thinking, "Well, that is easier said than done." No! It is easier than you think. As we continually bring our lives to Jesus on a daily basis, we remind ourselves that we cannot do anything apart from His help and His ability. Remaining in Jesus keeps us connected, at our most vital level, to His power causing it to flow freely into our lives. If you think about it for a minute, it is not as hard as we make it to remain. You just stay. You don't leave! You remain.

We never get too "mature" in God to ever stop connecting to

Him on this level. There will never be a day, as long as we live in our human bodies, that we won't need to be connecting our hearts to Jesus through His Word and time alone with Him in prayer. This is something we will never outgrow! Branches connected to the vine. This is what it means to remain, to be found in Him.

To Be like Him

One of the greatest dangers in not staying connected to Jesus is that we begin to lose sight of the goal of being like Him. We don't have to look very far to find someone or something to try and be like! Advertisers pray that people stay unhappy with themselves and their lives. They capitalize on poor self-esteem or poor self-image. Then they "create" a new image with whatever product they are selling. The same thing is true in media. It is easy to see the "perfection" presented to us through movies, TV, and social media and start to admire it, imitate it, and even crave it. When we admire someone, there is a quality we see in that person that we respect and value and usually want to develop in ourselves! Admiration is a good thing, but only to a certain extent. Admiration can turn into imitation when we start to identify with these qualities and begin to incorporate them into our own lives.

I have six nieces and one lone nephew on my side and two nephews on my husband's side! They are all close in age, and at the time of this writing, they have all entered the teenage space! They are so fun to be with as teenagers as they are becoming who they want to be. But I confess I miss them being little sometimes too. One of my favorite things when they were little was to be around them and watch them grow up! It was hilarious to watch their reactions as they would watch one of their favorite movies at that time in their little lives! As soon as the movie ends, my nieces especially would want to *become* the movie! It was hilarious! Somebody would become the director and divide up all the roles and parts of the various characters. And then it was ON! They do their best to be "just like her!" Or the boys, "just like him!" They would watch some movies over and over so many times that there is no way (in their minds) they can fail at this. They imitate every move and quote every line and know every song! They even want to be called by the name of the character they are portraying. They really believe they can be just like their favorite character in the movie! It is the best!

Admiration and imitation are not negative things! Many of the things we are imitating are the things we value in another person and may be the very things we need in our own lives. The fact that we begin to imitate some trait or behavior we see in another person's life can be a positive thing for us along the way! It's called influence. It's called having a role model! The problem for some people, however, is when a healthy admiration or imitation of another person doesn't stop. It goes too far. It moves beyond a harmless moment or period (like when my nieces and nephew watch a movie, playact for a short time, and then go on with their day) to a full-blown fantasy. This misplaced identity is generally the result of discontentment with who that person is and where they are in life!

This is not the case when it comes to imitating *Jesus* or wanting to be like *Him*. When it comes to Jesus, we *want* to be *discontent* with who we are without Him. We *want* an identity shift from who *we* are to *who* He is! Paul said it this way when he wrote, "I want to know Christ—yes, to know the power of his resurrection and participation in his sufferings, *becoming like him* in his death, and so, somehow, attaining to the resurrection from the dead" (Philippians 3:10–11, NIV).

When the goal is to be like Jesus, and we get a revelation about who He really is, we stop looking to become other people in order to try to be like them! Instead, we start to imitate the life of Jesus. Again, Paul writes in 2 Corinthians 3:18 (NIV), "And we all, who with unveiled faces contemplate the Lord's glory, are being *transformed into his image* with ever-increasing glory, which comes from the Lord." We begin to look like Jesus!

In order to be able to reflect the Lord's glory, however, it means we have to be looking at Him! In order to see our reflection in a mirror, we have to actually be standing in front of the mirror! The same is true with our spiritual reflection. The more we study Jesus, the more clearly we will see and understand ourselves. Our lives will become aligned with the way He made us to be! Our identity is no longer a question or something we can pick and choose based on our preferences, or what people say we should feel fine being, or anything society offers up as an identity option. It becomes certain and solid. I am who *He* says I am. I identify with Jesus. This happens over time and as a result of time spent with

Him. In other words, it doesn't happen all at once! Instead, as we continue to look at Jesus and become familiar with His features, something amazing happens: we become LIKE Him! The more time we spend in His presence, the more we start to recognize His voice. Our lives become a reflection of what we find in that time with Him. My life begins to match the message that I read in the Bible.

God doesn't want our life's goal to be some cheap version of what we thought was valuable here on the earth. The things God values most are the things that are unseen! The world looks with contempt at what we have acquired or achieved because there is always someone with more or who has achieved more. But Jesus? Jesus doesn't look at our outward appearance. He doesn't care how much or how little we have or what clothes we wear. Or what car we drive and where we live and what we do for a living. Jesus only cares about what is going on deep inside of us. He wants access to what is *real*. "So we fix our eyes not on what is seen, but on what is unseen, since what is seen is temporary, but what is unseen is eternal" (2 Corinthians 4:18, NIV). What is "seen" right now is so fleeting. As soon as it comes, it's on the way out! Jesus is far more concerned about what is eternal. What is lasting and what remains.

When our prayer is to be more like Jesus, He trains our eyes to stop looking at what is seen! Through the Holy Spirit, we begin to see into the unseen realm. We begin to see the eternal. As we pray to be more like Jesus, our perspective changes. The more time we spend in His presence, the more He shines His light into our spirit. He enables us to see the difference between the temporary things of this world and the things that will endure forever! In our goal-driven world, where our lives are so quickly sized up and defined by standards God never set, God wants us to focus on Jesus. He wants us to have the assurance and peace that comes from a life that is centered on Him! By remaining in Jesus, we will, without a doubt, become like Him.

The heart of God is for every single person to have a real relationship with Jesus Christ. Not a Sunday, holiday, or conference relationship, but a real encounter that will bring hunger to know Him in the everyday. God is gathering men and women all over the world who will desire more of Him so that they can serve Him at a higher level! Will you come? God's plan for your life goes beyond anything you can imagine! He wants to equip your life with more of His power so that He can use you to bring many people to Himself. If you are willing, then truly, there is nothing God won't be able to do with your life! There is an invitation that is going out from heaven every single day to come out INTO THE DEEP and seek the Lord until He comes. "And now, dear children, *continue* in him, so that when he appears we may be *confident* and *unashamed* before him at his coming" (1 John 2:28, NIV). "The Spirit and the bride [the church, the believers] say, 'Come!' And let the one who hears say, 'Come!' Let the one who is thirsty come; and let the one who wishes take the free gift of the water of life" (Revelation 22:17, NIV).

LAUNCHING POINT CHAPTER 10

- In your life, what have you considered to be, or imagined would be, your "great reward"?

- After reading chapter 10, what would you say needs to be shifted in your life so that you can truly say Jesus is your exceedingly great reward?

- How has this chapter changed your thinking? What do you need to do now as a result of this change?

WORKS CITED

Christ for all Nations. n.d. "Evangelist Reinhard Bonnke Biography." accessed April 18, 2023. https://cfan.org/reinhard-bonnke.

Exploring Our Fluid Earth. n.d. "Pressure." Accessed April 18, 2023. https://manoa.hawaii.edu/exploringourfluidearth/physical/ocean-depths/pressure.

Gibb, Natalie. 2019. "Factors Affecting Visibility Underwater When Scuba Diving." *LiveAbout*. January 30, 2019. https://www.liveabout.com/factors-that-affect-visibility-underwater-2963268

Persecution.org. 2006. "Persecution of Christians on the Rise." June 27, 2006. https://www.persecution.org/2006/06/28/persecution-of-christians-on-the-rise/

Ten Boom, Corrie. 1982. *Clippings from My Notebook*. Nashville, TN: Thomas Nelson, Inc.

Tulchinsky, Theodore H. 2018. "John Snow, Cholera, the Broad Street Pump; Waterborne Diseases Then and Now." *Case Studies in Public Health* (2018): 77–99. https://doi.org/10.1016%2FB978-0-12-804571-8.00017-2.

PRAYER TO GIVE JESUS YOUR LIFE

In the book of Revelation, Jesus says, "Here I am! I stand at the door and knock. If anyone hears my voice and opens the door, I will come in and eat with that person, and they with me" (Revelation 3:20, NIV). If you have never opened your heart's door to Jesus, today can be the day that you open that door and receive the FREE GIFT of salvation. There is nothing we can do to earn the great love of Jesus or our way to heaven. Jesus paid the price in full when He died on the cross for our sins. There is no sin that is too horrible for Jesus to forgive. No matter what you have done, Jesus invites you to come to Him! The Bible tells us in Romans that "ALL" have sinned and fall short of the glory of God. We all need a Savior.

The Bible says that TODAY is the day of salvation! We are not guaranteed tomorrow. God has given you this moment, right now, to decide to make your peace with Him and give Jesus your life. You don't need to wait another minute for your life in Jesus to begin.

The Bible tells us in Romans 10:9 (NIV), "If you declare with your mouth, 'Jesus is Lord,' and believe in your heart that God raised him from the dead, you will be saved."

If you want to receive Jesus for the first time, or if you know you are away from God and want to come home, just pray this simple prayer with me. You can do this right now, wherever you are.

Lord Jesus,

Today I come to You, I have heard Your knocking, and I open my heart's door to You now. I believe that You love me. I believe that You died for me. I know I'm a sinner, and I need Your forgiveness. Today I choose to follow You and give You control of my life. Right now, I declare that I believe in my heart, and I confess with my mouth that, Jesus, YOU ARE LORD and that God has raised You from the dead! I am now a Christian; Christ Jesus, YOU live in me. Help me to live for You and serve You all the days of my life.

In the name of Jesus, I pray.
Amen

If you just prayed this prayer, I would love to hear from you. Feel free to reach out to me through my website at www.bethanylentzmurdock.com. Also, be sure to tell someone you know. Maybe the person who gave you this book. I also want to encourage you to find a church in your area that preaches the Bible fully and will help you with your next steps in following Jesus. WELCOME HOME. We are family now! May God bless you and keep you and FILL you to overflow.

Bethany xx

ABOUT THE AUTHOR

Bethany is a board-certified master life foundations coach, carrying credentials through both the American Association of Christian Counselors and the International Christian Coaching Institute. She serves on the International Board of Reference as both a mentoring coach and lead coach trainer to upcoming coaches who seek credentialing through ICCI. Bethany serves global, national, and local clients both on an individual basis as well as in group settings. She also offers leadership training for churches and ministries. She is a dynamic speaker and preacher of the Word. She is an ordained worship and executive pastor. Bethany has her own coaching practice and lives in Virginia Beach, Virginia, with her husband, Paul, and their tiny Chihuahua, Jemmy. For more information, please visit www.bethanylentzmurdock.com.

CPSIA information can be obtained
at www.ICGtesting.com
Printed in the USA
JSHW012101220723
45087JS00004B/10